Theory as the Most Practical of All Things

Theory as the Most Practical of All Things

Theory Applications in Contemporary Practice

M. Scott Norton

ROWMAN & LITTLEFIELD
Lanham • Boulder • New York • London

Published by Rowman & Littlefield
An imprint of The Rowman & Littlefield Publishing Group, Inc.
4501 Forbes Boulevard, Suite 200, Lanham, Maryland 20706
www.rowman.com

6 Tinworth Street, London SE11 5AL, United Kingdom

Copyright © 2020 by M. Scott Norton

All rights reserved. No part of this book may be reproduced in any form or by any electronic or mechanical means, including information storage and retrieval systems, without written permission from the publisher, except by a reviewer who may quote passages in a review.

British Library Cataloguing in Publication Information Available

Library of Congress Cataloging-in-Publication Data Available

Library of Congress Control Number: 2020940815

ISBN 978-1-4758-5506-7 (cloth : alk. paper)
ISBN 978-1-4758-5507-4 (pbk. : alk. paper)
ISBN 978-1-4758-5508-1 (electronic)

Contents

Theory Preface ix

1 Theoretical Concepts Over the Years: What Theory Is and
   What It Is Not 1
   The Nature of Theory: What It Is and What It Isn't 2
   The Long Road toward Theory Development 4
   What Theory Is Not 5
   The Confusion between Theory and Axiology 6
   What about Philosophy and Its Relation, if Any, to Theory? 7
   One More Example of What Theory Is Not 7
   What Do Administrative Authorities Say About Theory? 7
   Theory Begins to Rise in Educational Administration 8
   How Does Theory Serve the Practicing School Administrator? 9
   Theory Can Serve as a Foundation for Administrative/Teacher
      Improvement 10
   Theory as a Guide for Decision-Making 11
   How Is Theory Developed? 11
   Further Thoughts on the Benefits of Theory 13
   Multiple Choice Questions 16
   Answers to the Quiz—True or False 16
   Your Score on the Quiz 17
   Answers to the Quiz: Multiple Choice 18
   Key Chapter Ideas and Recommendations 18
   Discussion Questions 19
   References 19

2	Educational Theories of the Scientific Management Era and Their Presence in Contemporary Practice	21
	Frederick Taylor's Scientific Management Concepts	22
	A Description of the Scientific Management Era	22
	Rationalistic Leadership and Scientific Management as promoted by Frederick Taylor	23
	Scientific Management and Educational Practices	26
	Scientific Management and School Administration	27
	Henri Fayol and His Fourteen Principles of Management	28
	Henri Fayol's Contributions to Scientific Management	28
	Max Weber and His Early Contributions to Administrative Leadership	33
	The Characteristics of Administrative Leadership	34
	The Impact of Efficiency on Educational Practices	34
	Gantt Charts: Established in the Early 1900 and Used Commonly Today in Education	36
	Much More about Efficiency	37
	Emerson's Twelve Principles of Efficiency	38
	The Twelve Principles of Efficiency as Contended by Emerson	38
	Examples of Efficiency as Set Forth during the Scientific Management Era	40
	An Early Concept of Defined Ideas Related to Business Administration	41
	The Creative Efficiency Concept of Henry R. Towne	41
	Continued: Additional Concepts Set Forth in the Scientific Management Era	42
	Answers to the Quiz	44
	Scientific Management Still Endures in Education: An Analysis by Maduakolam Ireh-2016	44
	Key Chapter Ideas and Recommendations	46
	Discussion Questions	47
	References	48
3	The Theories and Concepts of the Human Relations Era: Their Influence on Contemporary Practice	49
	Follett's Four Principles of Coordination	50
	The Importance of Coordination Today and in the Future	50
	Elton Mayo's Famous Hawthorne Experiments Regarding the Motives of the Worker?	51
	The Importance of the Human Factor Leads the Way for Organizational Improvement	52
	The Needs of Workers, Human Motivation, and Human Relations	53

Contents vii

Motivation as a Pursuit toward One's Goals	57
The Motivational Concepts Set Forth by Herzberg: Motivators and Hygienes	57
Motivators and Hygienes for Teachers and Administrators	58
One More Look at Motivation in Terms of Theory X and Theory Y	59
Chester Barnard and His "Best Book" for Educational Administration	59
Etzioni and the Compliance Theory	60
Vroom's Motivational Model: Expectancy, Instrumentality, and Valence	60
Motivational Theory: Vroom's Expectancy Theory	62
Hanlon's Theorem 21: Energy Is Released in Proportion to Perceived Involvement	63
Goal-Path Motivation: A "First Cousin" of Hanlon's Theorem 21	64
Human Relations and Leadership Styles	65
A Focus on Selected Theories/Concepts and Their Influence on Contemporary Practices	66
Lost and Found: Vygotsky's Theory on Cognitive Development	67
The Influence of the Human Relations Era: The Era Itself Had Major Influences on Contemporary Practices in Education	68
A Break for a Multiple Choice Quiz	68
The Answers to the Foregoing Multiple Choice Quiz	70
Key Chapter Ideas and Recommendations	72
Discussion Questions	73
References	73

4 Postmodernism: Behavioral Science and the Reconstructionist Movement — 75

The Great Influence of the Social Systems Model of 1957	76
Systems Theory: Structure and Relationships	77
Attention! A Light Bulb Experience	77
Theories and Concepts for the Field of Administrative Leadership	78
Transactional Leadership and Contemporary Practices	79
A Summary of Leadership Types in Practice	80
Attempts to Assess the Various Leadership Styles	81
Rensis Likert's Four-Style Leadership Concepts	81
A Look at System 4-T: The Best of the Best	82
Principal Turnover: So What?	83
Fiedler and Chemers's Contingency Leadership Model	83
Etzioni's Compliance Theory: Stimulation toward Commitment	84
The Fifth Dimension: Peter Seng's Focus on the Learning Organization	85

Gareth Morgan and Single- and Double-Loop Learning	86
Organizational Success with Five Central Characteristics: Critical Thinking of Michael Fullan	87
New Days and New Ways toward Organizational Effectiveness	88
Likert's System 4-T Organization—a Step Higher Than System 4	89
Theories and Concepts Related to Student Learning Styles	89
Competency-Based Programming: Learning Not Time is the Basic Feature	91
Whatever Happened to the ISLLC Standards for School Leaders?	93
Measurements and Formulas for Determining Results	94
What Constitutes Teacher Load?	94
Concluding Comments	95
Key Chapter Ideas and Recommendations	96
Discussion Questions: Self-Assessments	98
References	98
About the Author	101

Theory Preface

WHY THIS BOOK WAS WRITTEN

When asked the question as to the effectiveness of their preparation program in the fields of teaching and educational administration, the common reply was that the programs were too theoretical and did not directly relate to the knowledge and skills needed for success in the real world of education. Respondents expressed the need for more direct experience and practice in the field. The belief that being able to observe a great teacher in the classroom or serving as an intern alongside a highly effective school administrator would have served potential educators in a better way. Theory about how to organize a school program or how to motivate a classroom of students commonly is viewed as falling short of what is needed to be successful in the field.

In addition, the views of theory are often mistaken. All too often theory is viewed as someone's opinion about what should be done or simply the guesswork of someone regarding best practices. In addition, theory commonly is confused with other terms such as axiologies, paradigms, taxonomies, and even philosophies.

In reality, a valid and reliable theory is based on a serious implementation of scientific observations that ultimately lead to certain conclusions about relationships that result when they are seriously assessed and evaluated over time. When the observed results occur time after time, a strong belief about the relationships takes place and a hypothesis is developed relative to what is observed. The hypothesis is set forth and then tested and re-tested. Ultimately, testing results permit the development of a tentative theory that is once again assessed and evaluated in many different ways. Ultimately, the observations and implementation results are such that the term theory can be applied. Eventually, new hypotheses and new theories are likely to be developed from the information now in place.

The foregoing paragraph is to underscore the fact that a valid and reliable theory is supported by a scientific process that includes a long period of observation, scientific examination, implementation, and practice. Authorities have set forth the belief that theory is the most practical of all things. Theory can be of paramount value to the practicing educational teacher and administrator. The contents of this book set forth the many primary benefits of theory for education in general and professional practice specifically. In addition, the importance of including high levels of research and theory implementation in practice is supported throughout the book.

HOW THE BOOK IS ORGANIZED

The book includes four chapters that include an in-depth discussion of theory as to what it is and what it is not. Chapter 1 centers on defining the term *theory* and differentiating it from such concepts as axiologies, paradigms, taxonomies, and philosophy. Chapter 2 sets forth many of the theories that were set forth during the scientific management era headed by Frederick Taylor. The chapter points out that many of the theories developed during this era did not evolve from the field of education but were primarily directed to the fields of business and industrial management. Nevertheless, such theories commonly were believed to hold benefits for educational practices and were readily accepted by leaders of that field as well.

Chapter 3 centers on the human relations era that fostered a new look at administrative management. The concepts that "organizations are people" and that the human factor was of great importance for organizational success were addressed in a wide variety of ways many of which were led by Mary Parker Follett who was considered by many as the leader in the development of effective management practices. For example, the concepts of cooperation/collaboration, which are among the leading topics in contemporary discussions of organizational success, were among the leading topics during the human resources era.

Chapter 4 presents the theories and concepts of prime importance during the postmodern and reconstruction era. The topic of leadership dominated the topics of management, and a variety of leadership types were addressed during this time in history. In addition, the most effective leadership types were perceived in relation to their focus on administrative behavior and their human relationships. The terms democratic, heterarchial, transactional, competency-based, and aesthetic leadership were among those leadership styles that were set forth as being most effective in practice. Participative leadership loomed as important as well.

The book is of special importance for those persons serving in administrative roles in higher education. Practicing school leaders will find ample opportunities to assess and evaluate their own style of leadership with the leadership theories addressed in the book. Those individuals aspiring to leadership roles in education will find the contents of the book as a valuable source of information as they advance into the important work of educational administration and supervision. Teaching personnel will also benefit by the theory information relative to human motivation, learning styles, human cooperation, human relationships, learning culture, teacher load, and other concepts of educational practices that have developed over many decades.

HOW THIS BOOK IS ORGANIZED

The four chapters of the book include the major educational controversies/debates that are being encountered presently in local school education. Chapter 1 centers on the controversial educational issues being encountered at the local school level and the debates that tend to inhibit school success. The number of controversial issues at the local level is so extensive that the second chapter also is devoted to issues at the local school level. Chapter 3 focuses on the educational controversies that are primarily a concern of the various states. Chapter 4 focuses on the many controversial education issues being encountered at the federal level of our nation. In each chapter of the book, the nature of the controversies/debates that are present is discussed along with the pro and con statements that underscore the opinion differences that exist among the educators and general citizenry.

Whenever valid and reliable research is available on any issue being discussed, it is included in the discussion. The content does point out, however, the lack of scientific and empirical research in many areas of educational practice. Improved educational research practices at all levels of government are viewed as a significant need for resolving many of the controversies that remain unresolved. The need for extensive educational research is noted throughout the book. In addition, the fact is that mostly every educational controversy is present within all three levels of government: local, state, and federal.

All educators, school board members, state department education officials, federal education department personnel, parents, and the nation's general citizenry will find this book engaging and of interest. Professors in education departments should have the book in their professional libraries. Many different courses in education will find the book to be a valuable supplementary resource.

Chapter 1

Theoretical Concepts Over the Years
What Theory Is and What It Is Not

Primary chapter goal: To present the facts relative to the influential concepts that have been implemented in education historically. Differentiating among and between various concepts is detailed. What is theory and how theory benefits practice are given primary attention.

What primary theories and other educational concepts have had significant influence on educational practices? Is theory nothing more than someone's guesswork, a shot in the dark relative to what someone thinks about a matter or is there any evidence that such concepts serve an important role in supporting educational program effectiveness? Chapter 1 centers on the examination of theory and other educational concepts in relation to how they are developed and what role they may have played in the matters of educational practices. We discuss factors that have contributed to the confusion of theory such as a taxonomy, axiology, philosophy, paradigm, and postulational thinking.

Various theories are set forth and commonly presented in various preparation programs for use by the practitioner. Some theories come to the front for a time and then fade with the ever-changing times. Some theories remain in practice and others are extended by new hypothesis and observations. Although not always placed into practice with its specific name, the theoretical concept remains and its contentions commonly come to be the way things are done in practice.

Practitioners often implement theoretical concepts without knowing or using their original name. For example, school leaders might implement program activities in relation to students' best interests and needs. Theories related to the work of Montessori or Piaget center on such provisions. Or the administrator might design educational activities accompanied by student motivational rewards and other learning enhancements. In such instances, the motivational concepts of Skinner and other authorities, as discussed in this chapter, are being implemented in practice.

Theory is given primary consideration in this chapter since it has the potential of serving educational practices in important ways. In addition, considerable attention is given to other concepts that have influenced practices in business and industry, and in turn, have impacted practices in education as well. However, the primary focus of this book is investigating the various concepts to examine their "staying power"; that is, how many and to what extent have the many theories influenced contemporary practices? Chapters 2, 3, and 4 are devoted to answering that question.

THE NATURE OF THEORY: WHAT IT IS AND WHAT IT ISN'T

We approach this topic with the hypothesis that any field that expects to move ahead must have a theoretical framework. Therefore, as John Dewey (1929) stated, "Theory in the end is the most practical of all things because the widening of the range of attention beyond nearby purposes and desire eventually results in the creation of farther and wider-reaching purposes, and enables us to make use of a much wider range of conditions and means than were expressed in the observation of primitive practical purposes" (p. 17).

Implications of Dewey's remarks underscore the fact that the need of the administrator is a practical approach that sets forth techniques and answers for problems and situations encountered in the field. Certainly, the practice of administration necessitates the solution of practical problems; yet, a prescriptive approach that seemingly provides the ways to solve specific problems in the field most often serves as a stop-gap measure at best.

Jacob Getzels and others (1968) have noted that the so-called practical approach actually solves few of the problems faced by the educator due to the many questions that such a strategy requires. For example, which suggested approach should be used? Is there one "best bet" among all the many suggestions that come to mind? What is to be done next if the chosen suggestion does not work; just choose another one?

As Getzels (1968) and others have noted, "To be sure theories without practices like maps without routes may be empty, but practices without routes, like theory without maps, are blind" (pp. 8–9). A cookbook approach to any organizational practices simply will be unsatisfactory.

It is necessary to understand that the development of theory is not a "simple" activity. On the contrary, theory development commonly is a complex activity that is developed creatively over a long period of time. The following information is presented with the primary purpose of underscoring the fact that theory is not just an expression of someone's beliefs. Rather, it is developed through a complex of observation and assessment activities that serve to test a problematic situation of some importance. Several specific examples are discussed in relation to answering the question of "what theory is not."

What is the answer, then, to this dilemma? The need for the organizational leader is a way to define and/or analyze a problem or situation being encountered; a guide for gathering appropriate information and a means which serves to provide a range of ideas for possible action and a foundation for extending personal knowledge and wisdom toward the resolution of the problem at hand. Hoy and Miskel (2001) summarized the value of theory for the practitioner as being the ultimate function to provide general explanations for phenomena. In order to do this, theory has a more specific function—to guide empirical research and present an integrating and common framework for the development of knowledge.

Theory serves to guide action as it provides the bases for making decisions about questions and problems encountered in practice. Concepts and theories enable the practitioner to make sense out of the complexities of reality and thus provide strategic and rational actions for resolving the problems being faced. It provides a framework from which to describe behavior and to guide research. Through research, theory is ultimately transformed into practice. Given the mutually beneficial association of these concepts, it appears that neither theory nor raw empiricism can survive alone.

Simple remedies, intuition, and common sense are simply too limited to deal with the complex social, moral, and political issues being faced. These forms of thought are viewed as being "situation" bound and thus they tend to leave gaps in one's understanding. Theoretical premises must be understood not only as a set of logically interrelated propositions, but also as a way of perceiving and interpreting an aspect of reality. The administrator who keeps abreast of theory will benefit by being able to widen and deepen his or her understanding toward, what Dewey has termed, "nearby purposes." As a result, the practitioner will gain a wider and deeper understanding of the many problems and situation being faced.

The term theory elicits different meanings in the minds of individuals. For example, studies have revealed that such descriptive words as impractical, speculation, and philosophy have been used by administrators and others as being synonymous with theory. The implications, of course, are that many individuals relate theory to philosophizing outside the realm of reality or to some kind of guesswork resulting from aimless speculation.

On the contrary, viable theory is closely related to a fact-founded approach which serves to extend knowledge and understanding on a logical and scientific basis. In order to understand theory, it needs to be examined. In a mathematics subject such as geometry, for example, certain propositions or hypotheses are proven through the use of logical arguments. Basic assertions or axioms, which are accepted at the outset without proof, serve as the basis for arguments. If a hypothesis is found to be valid through the testing procedures utilized and when several hypotheses serve to support a generalization or when the hypothesis serves to explain phenomena generally in a given field, the term theory is applied.

In some instances, the word law is used interchangeable with theory and in educational administration the term principle sometimes is used in the same context. In each case, the inference is that a theory statement reflects an acceptable conclusion. Theories, then, represent valid conclusions which have been generalized on the basis of logical arguments or the testing of hypotheses. New theories, in turn, serve as the basis for new hypotheses and further extension of theory leads to new knowledge.

THE LONG ROAD TOWARD THEORY DEVELOPMENT

A theory is developed commonly through knowledgeable observation. The process begins by observing what is seen, what is heard, and what is happening. These observations, in a collective way of reasoning and rationale, lead to various inferences relative to what is actually taking place. Through these inferences, some tentative hypotheses are developed which are tested by way of further observation and experimentation for the purpose of developing further confidence in their validity.

Such activity commonly results in the ability to develop generalizations about the phenomena in the particular field being observed. These generalizations remain tentative and are re-tested, taken apart, put back together. If they hold true over a period of time and added confidence is found in the results, it is reasonable to state that a theory has begun to be developed.

When the theory is confirmed, testing through repeated experimentation and applications in practice is planned and developed. Since the new testing might lead to a different concept of that theory, it is held tentatively. New inferences and hypotheses might be developed and the cycle of theory development begins all over again. The foregoing "complex" description of theory development hopefully will set aside any thoughts of theory as a contention held by someone about some method or practice or an opinion based on one's experience over the years.

Several other definitions have been set by "scientists" that view theory as a set of assumptions from which a larger set of empirical laws are delivered using logical mathematical procedures. Theory has been viewed as a logically developed body of confirmed generalizations whereby certain assumptions and concepts can be identified. It is true that theory has been viewed as the result of creative thinking about the problem/matter in relation to specific and systematic observations.

In addition, theory might be viewed as a hypothesis that has been thoroughly tested and has revealed the same results over a considerable period of time. The characteristics of observations, inferences, hypotheses, and generalizations are common to most all definitions and views leading to theory.

WHAT THEORY IS NOT

Sometimes it is helpful in attempting to define a term to consider what it is not. The terminology often used in relation to theory sometimes results in confusion or misuse of terms. A common problem is that of applying the term theory to a method, model, or perhaps a taxonomy. A *taxonomy* is an orderly classification according to presumed and natural relationships. While taxonomies become quite valuable in the classification of information related to various administrative processes, a taxonomy is limited and differs from a theory in that it does not provide an opportunity for extending knowledge scientifically.

A taxonomy can be of considerable value as an analytical framework for facilitating inquiry. For example, a taxonomy might serve as a scheme for classifying and/or suggesting existing relationships with regard to a set of phenomena. What taxonomy comes to mind almost immediately in this regard? Bloom's taxonomy (1956), in effect, says that those instructional objectives that are designed to seek only the acquisition of knowledge are the lowest level of both complexity and importance. The levels of comprehension, application, analysis, synthesis, and evaluation are next in line as being high or low in knowledge acquisition.

For example, knowledge is illustrated by defining words or naming the capitals of the fifty states. Comprehension follows in line when the learner is able to show the inflation escalation during a period of time on a line graph. Application would be illustrated by a student when he or she wrote an essay showing why education is not to be controlled at the federal level. The highest level of the taxonomy, evaluation, is illustrated when a student reads the novel, *The Fall of the House of Usher*, and is able to identify the underlying factor of incest.

Other well-known taxonomies include Gulick's and Urwick's (1937) POSDCoRB which sets forth the seven major functions of the administrator: planning, organization, staffing, directing, coordinating, reporting, and budgeting. In brief, taxonomies are useful in classification matters, handling large volumes of facts, and in some cases, can lead to thoughts about related theories.

Gulick's and Urwick's concepts are revealed in contemporary practices. Planning is ongoing in most every school program. Each of the other activities is being practiced by a variety of administrative staff personnel. The concepts of organization, coordinating, and reporting and budgeting are crucial activities at the local school level today.

THE CONFUSION BETWEEN THEORY AND AXIOLOGY

There also is considerable confusion between theory and axiology. Axiology commonly is defined as the study of the nature of value and the kinds of things that are valuable. In educational administration, there is a tendency to focus on how things ought to be. That is, an emphasis is placed on correcting human behavior rather than placing an emphasis on describing and analyzing actual administrative behavior. Thus, there is confusion of factual statements with value judgments. Questions of fact can be answered through scientific methods. However, questions of value cannot be verified through scientific inquiry.

The foregoing statements are to say that theory does not set forth the ethical path to follow or attempt to provide the answer as to what is good. Theory does serve to project the likely results of certain actions which the individual might pursue. In this respect, theory provides the foundation for the scientific aspects of an organization's administration. While the science of educational administration, for example, limits the insertion of ethics in the developments of its theory, many persons argue that the pluses of this objective are minuses as well in the area of actual practice.

This difficult situation has been addressed by Sergiovanni and others (1987) as they have noted that the problem of deciding which scientific propositions are appropriate for school administrators, for example, is additionally compounded due to the presence of unanticipated consequences of the various administrative acts. Thus, the administration might be scientific in that one can make fairly accurate predictions based on theory and propositions, but theory is also artistic in the sense that once action is implemented, the variability and complexity of human behavior produce unanticipated consequences that defy systematic decision-making.

While axiology is a consideration of importance in the study of organizational development, it is not the appropriate component of the scientific considerations which are concerned with fact as opposed to values or what ought to be.

WHAT ABOUT PHILOSOPHY AND ITS RELATION, IF ANY, TO THEORY?

Philosophy is another term frequently used as being synonymous with theory. Philosophy is concerned primarily with pursuits that led to answers as to what is real, what is true, and what is good. Considerations as to what is to be valued are the primary concerns of philosophy. This type of concern focuses on axiological kinds of considerations and is not theory. As previously noted, theory does not provide the practitioner with a set of values which is utilized to direct the leader toward actions which are good. Philosophy is more concerned with reality, truth, and values.

ONE MORE EXAMPLE OF WHAT THEORY IS NOT

A paradigm is viewed as a pattern of something such as a model, a pattern, or an example. Theory is not a model or the same as a paradigm. Models serve as a bridge between the purely abstract and the practical. An example of a paradigm is the social systems model of behavior set forth by Guba and Getzels (1957). This model states that social behavior may be understood as a function of three major elements: Instruction, role, and expectation which together constitute the nomothetic or normative dimension of activity in a social system. On the other hand, the individual personality and need disposition is termed the idiographic or human dimension of an organization.

WHAT DO ADMINISTRATIVE AUTHORITIES SAY ABOUT THEORY?

One of the most serious indictments of theory was stated in 1960 in a public address by Andrew Halpin. He stated an opinion that there does not exist today either in education or in industry a single well-developed theory of administration that is worth getting excited about. Today, in 2020, this indictment remains in place. Most knowledgeable persons of educational administration and students tend to agree that theory development in the field has been thin at best. Educational administration has tended to borrow various theories from the behavioral sciences and other areas and tried to make them applicable to the field of administration.

For example, the Herzberg theory of human motivation, that centered on job satisfaction, was derived outside the field of educational administration. Yet, more than 200 studies that related to the replication of the foregoing study had been reported in the early 1960s. As noted previously, educational personnel have tended to borrow theories from other disciplines to see how they apply to education as opposed to developing theory to extend knowledge in their own field.

It appears to be somewhat difficult to refer to a work by Chester Barnard in 1938 as a first serious effort toward implementing a theory approach to educational administration. This work was set forth approximately eight decades ago. Barnard was among the first to view organizations as consisting of the two dimensions of structural or formal dimension and a human or informal dimension. His ideas of cooperation and the three key functions of the organizational executive were forward looking administratively. He stated that every executive must be able to form the purposes of the organization, maintain effective communication in the organization, and obtain the necessary performance from members.

That is, commitment was essential for bringing members into a cooperative relationship and motivating them to surrender personal conduct in order achieve what he termed the *superordinate goals*. Barnard's early book, *The Functions of the Executive* (1938), has been viewed by many authorities as the most important book ever written in educational administration.

THEORY BEGINS TO RISE IN EDUCATIONAL ADMINISTRATION

Getzels and Guba (1957), Mort (1957), and others began to give some direction as to the value of theory and approaches to administration. The fact that there was little valid theory underlying the field of educational administration and these individuals and others were hopeful that their works would help turn the tide. In 1946, Paul Mort commented on his perspective of the search for theory in educational administration. That is, he expressed his concern for the lack of theory in educational administration and the need of a search for useful theory in the field.

Hanlon (1968), former professor at Marquette University, underscored a major problem regarding the lack of theory development and implementation in educational practices. As stated by Hanlon:

I have taught the resulting theory of self-actualization for several years now to graduate and undergraduate students of education and to graduate students of administration. I have also taught it to practicing administration students of education and education lack an understanding of what theory really is. The closely net of postulates and theorems which characterize theory the basic set of generalizations has been made available to guide reading and discussion. The mastery of the form brings rather amazing results: the second philosophy and social science preparation (p. iv). As a result of all this ferment, in the early 1950s, the 1954 conference concerning "where we are in the development of theory" was held in Denver, Colorado. A follow-up conference goal of theory development in the field.

However, in 1968, a book by Hanlon was styled along the lines of postulational thinking. Each chapter set forth various postulates that serve to establish theorems in the field of administration. Although the book promoted the development of various theories in the field of educational administration, the work did little to promote the wave of theory throughout the field.

Why has theory made little progress in the field of administration? Some authorities have mentioned the serious lack of research methodology in the field. Serious questions have been raised about the nature of research that has taken place in education. For example, Ed Bridges of Stanford University noted that over the last several years more than 90 percent of the research in educational administration has relied on the survey method of research using only a single instrument for collecting the data; the infamous questionnaire or a single factor correctional without controls in data analysis.

In addition, researchers who studied educational administration manifested little interest in practical problems and theoretically oriented research activities were virtually nonexistent in doctoral dissertation studies.

HOW DOES THEORY SERVE THE PRACTICING SCHOOL ADMINISTRATOR?

How does theory actually serve the practitioner? In no field of endeavor has real progress been made without theory. Theory can be useful to the school administrator in providing direction and meaning to the work performed. Specifically, a theory can serve many benefits: problem analysis; administrators must be able to discern the problems in situations that they encounter. This skill involves the ability to conceptualize the specific situations as well as knowing what information is necessary to resolve the problem(s) being faced.

For example, several writers have theorized in the area of related orientation which is characterized by job accomplishment through technical job effectiveness. Role orientation emphasizes responsibilities of the specific job. What does the job description say relative to the specific knowledge and requirements for effective performance? Is there a conflict between what is viewed as task orientation versus role orientation? The organization is concerned with the task and the worker is concerned with their job role. Severe conflicts might be avoided through proper attention to problem analysis and strategies that alleviate the inevitable conflict.

Effective theory should also serve as a guide for administrative action. The decision-making process involves evaluation of alternative choices with each choice having its own set of probable consequences. Theory can serve as a guide for thinking through the likely consequences of actions that are taken. Assume, for example, that the general orientation of the employee group is that of task. We note that technical effectiveness is the key ingredient of that orientation. The persons with the most knowledge and expertise take over the leadership responsibilities since that expertise is the key at the time to complete the given task requirements.

Since such an orientation also undergirds employee motivation through satisfaction in the excellence of work and commitment to the task, administrative decisions necessarily should be made with these considerations clearly in mind. Decision about work tasks based on other role orientations, such as personal needs and sole judgments of subordinates in the organization, would have negative consequences at best.

THEORY CAN SERVE AS A FOUNDATION FOR ADMINISTRATIVE/TEACHER IMPROVEMENT

Since theory does provide a basis for problem analysis and as a guide for administrative action, it can serve as a sounding board for the viability of administrative behavior and practice as well. Working within a specific theoretical framework, the administration can evaluate the results of actions in a critical and purposeful way. Adjustments in the behavior therefore become purposeful and preferred results become more possible. In the same manner, revisions in the theoretical framework utilized can be determined and retested for viability in specific situations.

Adjustments in one's personal behavior and in the theory in question itself might be needed in view of the end results that come about. The theory provides a framework for action as opposed to a "fight the fire" approach. One major consideration is the application of theory. Consider the important factor of worker motivation. Herzberg and others (1959) set forth a major hypothesis that considers the factors leading to positive attitudes toward work and those leading to negative attitudes. That is, do different factors bring about job satisfaction than those factors that bring about dissatisfaction? Herzberg found that the factors do differ.

The hypothesis was tested with groups of engineers and accountants at the outset. Since that time, the theory has been tested with virtually every kind of work group including teachers, principals, and others. The first five factors that were associated with job satisfaction were achievement, recognition, work itself, responsibility, and advancement. These terms were given the name "motivators." Factors such as job security, personal life considerations, working conditions, company policy, and technical supervision were not associated with job satisfaction but found to be important factors of job dissatisfaction.

In teaching, educational theory sets forth the rationale for designing instruction that is most effective for student learning. Theories serve to give the teacher more confidence in the instructional methods/strategies used in the classroom.

THEORY AS A GUIDE FOR DECISION-MAKING

Consider an organization whose morale and overall worker satisfaction is unsatisfactory. What would be the first considerations for the practicing administrator? The need would be to remove the dissatisfaction by emphasizing the improvement of the hygiene factors (i.e., company policy, technical supervision, salary, interpersonal relations, interpersonal relations with subordinates, and working conditions) and then to implement major improvements by implementing motivators such as worker achievement, recognition, work itself, responsibility, advancement, and salary. To work on motivators alone would not remove the negative level of dissatisfaction that is in place.

HOW IS THEORY DEVELOPED?

It has been noted that theory is based on valid conclusions that have been derived from logical thinking and various tests of hypotheses that have been determined. A *hypothesis* is a statement that has resulted from the relationships observed between existing variables. A theory is developed initially by a persistent process of *observations*. The relationships, behaviors, and physical developments are observed commonly over long periods of time. The results of such *observations*, along with reasoning about what is observed, lead to various *inferences* based on increased understanding and logical reasoning as to what has taken place (see figure 1.1).

Thus, an *inference* is a conclusion reached on the basis of evidence and reasoning. Related synonyms of the term, inference, would include hypothesizing, deduction, speculation, and reasoning. As shown in figure 1.1, the results of preliminary inferencing lead to additional testing and experimenting. A

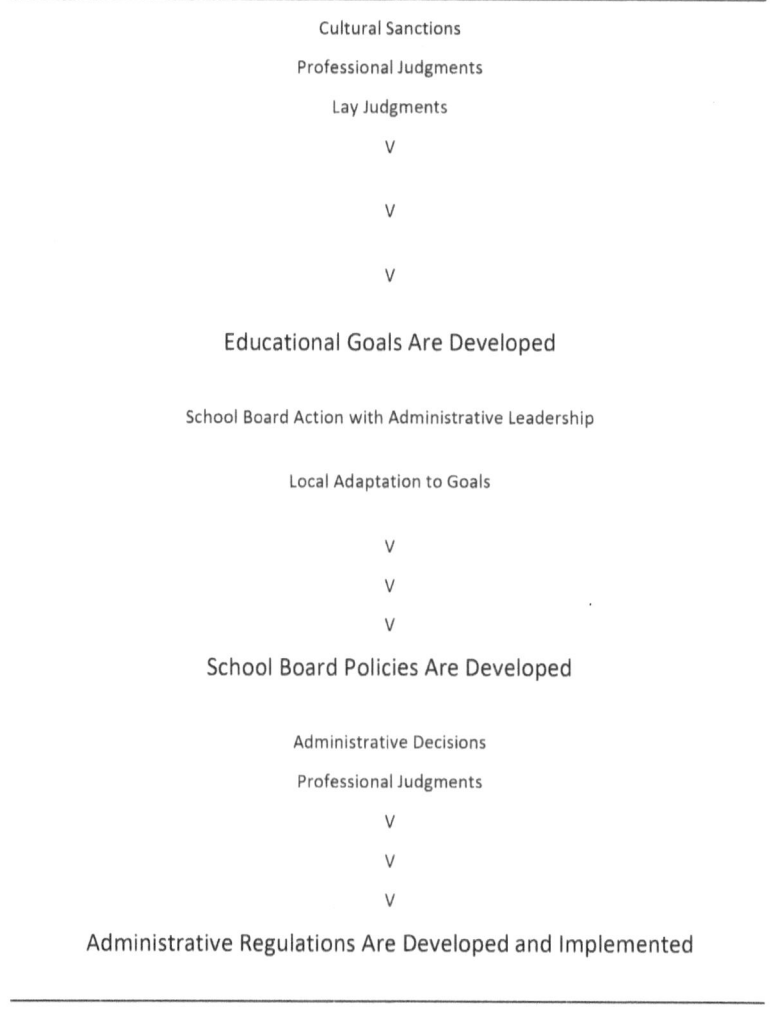

Figure 1.1   Conceptual Model of the Development of Goals, Policies and Administrative Regulations.

clear statement termed a *hypothesis* is set forth. That is, a statement is made that sets forth specifically what is to be investigated additionally. For example, what are the specific relationships between two or more variables? An "if this, then this" statement is studied from a scientific point of view (e.g., in the case of two variables, do Zs that are added to Ys get better results than Zs that are not added to Ys?).

From the hypothesis statement, additional testing takes place, including measuring and reasoning. Results are observed commonly over long periods of time. Additional confidence is gained as various applications are found to be valid. Confirmed testing leads to a *generalization* and to other hypotheses which are sometimes termed principles or laws. In turn, the developed theory serves to begin new observations and ultimately new hypotheses and new knowledge.

The foregoing information is intended to underscore the nature of a theory and the "scientific involvement" that accompanies its development. Thus, theory is much more than someone's guesswork or an untested idea that is not based on scientific measures. Without such theory, there is virtually no foundation for knowledge.

Figure 1.2 A Model of Theory Development.

OBSERVATION—Many observations of variables of behavior and physical phenomena over long periods of time are activated----->INFERENCES—Reasoning about what is observed is recorded and analyzed-------->HYPOTHESIS-----A statement of what is to be investigated is set forth in detail------>GENERALIZATION---Additional testing and experimenting with applications continues; results are validated------->THEORY----A valid theory is confirmed for implementation in practice. Scientific research often leads to improved practices. New and extended hypotheses commonly occur that lead to new hypotheses, new theories, and established law.

FURTHER THOUGHTS ON THE BENEFITS OF THEORY

There are several reasons why the practitioner should give serious thought to educational theory. One characteristic of great teachers and administers is that they "insist" on opportunities to grow and develop. If such opportunities are not available in their present work activities, these talented persons tend to seek employment elsewhere. Three specific benefits of theory for the practicing leader are of paramount importance.

Benefit number one is that valid theory can serve to guide the individual in analyzing existing problems. That is, theory does not tell the individual what or how to do something, rather it points up what is likely to happen if certain action is or is not taken. This information, coupled with the individual's personal values and ethics of the individual along with his or her professional beliefs and experience, results in the benefit of answering the question of what should be done.

Mostly every model for effective decision-making opens with the step of gathering important information for clarifying and answering the question/problem at hand. Theory gives the leader the direction necessary for gathering the important information. The decision-making step of gathering/clarifying the problem commonly leaves the door open by stating "gather all the facts" relative to the matter at hand. First of all, when does the leader ever have time or the resources for gathering *all* the information relative to the matter? Theory gives the leader the best available guideline for completing this first important step in problem solving.

In addition, theory benefits the practitioner by explaining the nature of the work facing the school leader. For example, theory helps the leader in the examination of the relationships among and between the various components of the internal and external dimensions of the environment. It helps in the examination of the structural and human dimensions of the social system in which the school resides.

Educational supervisors and teachers are handicapped when they cannot adapt to the larger system purposes through learning. Management by objectives (MBO) is an example of one plan for the school that furthered certain concepts of scientific management. The MBO concept proposed that employees' motivation level would be increased if they jointly defined educational goals in terms of expected outcomes. More specifically, the concept was founded on the belief that employees would be more efficient and more productive if certain management practices were enforced. Examples of such practices are as follows:

Giving:

- the worker increased responsibility for developing personal goals in relation to the larger goals of the organization.
- the worker more autonomy in using their own creative talents for achieving them.
- attention to a variety of methods for evaluating the achievement of determined goals.

Such organizational concepts commonly do not escape criticism. Although MBO goals are viewed as being determined cooperatively by the worker and the supervisor, required standards and goals for the school program, overtime, entered the scene via state and federal requirements. Follow the mandated requirements or loose the funding that otherwise would be received. Educators are yet to find the solution to the concepts of providing an educational program based on the individual student's needs and interests and meeting the requirements of external agencies that set forth both the required educational standards and the methods that must be utilized for achieving them.

Lastly, theory can be instrumental in helping the practitioner toward his or her thinking about the work itself. The matters of leadership and organizational development, for example, can be examined in more depth than previously observed. Are we doing the right thing? Are we using the material and human resources available to us in the best and most creative way? What are the existing inhibitors and facilitators within our present program practices and what opportunities are being overlooked according to our theoretical assessments? As stated by Cleveland (1980), "The indispensable quality of leadership is the capacity to relate disparate 'facts' to the coherent theory, to fashion tactics that are part of a strategy, to act today in ways that are consistent with a studied view of the future" (p. 2).

A Quiz on Theory Development

Directions: Answer true or false to each of the following ten statements. Check your answers at the end of the quiz.

1. Theory is best defined as an expression or thought of someone's personal beliefs based on life's experiences. True ____ or False ____
2. Theory serves to guide action as it provides the bases for making decisions about questions and problems encountered in practice. True ____ or False ____
3. Theory is closely related to a fact-founded approach that serves to extend knowledge and understanding. True ____ or False ____
4. A theory is developed most commonly through knowledgeable observations. True ____ or False ____
5. A theory and a taxonomy or axiology are made of the same cloth. True ____ or False ____
6. Philosophy is a synonym for theory. True ____ or False ____
7. In spite of the ongoing criticism of public education's quality in K–12 schools, research efforts and related theory in the area of program development have been exemplary over the years. True ____ or False ____
8. Regardless of the criticism of educational progress, research within the profession has been of highest priority historically. True ____ or False ____
9. Theory in education has been a low priority due to its inability to serve as a foundation for administration improvement. True ____ or False ____
10. One cited benefit of theory for the practitioner is that it tells how to do something. True ____ or False ____

MULTIPLE CHOICE QUESTIONS

1. A theory is:
   a. a hunch held by an individual that in his or her mind in worthy of implementation
   b. the same as a hypothesis
   c. a statement or generalization that explains some phenomena in a systematic way
   d. the same as a philosophy
   e. synonymous with a taxonomy
2. A concept is:
   a. a term to which a particular meaning has been attached (leadership, morale)
   b. a generalization
   c. an hypothesis
   d. a taxonomy
   e. none of the above
3. What term below is closest to a taxonomy?
   a. truth
   b. generalization
   c. hypothesis
   d. paradigm
   e. orderly classification
4. Which one word below would best describe or reflect Taylor's scientific management task system?
   a. coordination
   b. esprit de corps
   c. efficiency
   d. linking pins
   e. need dispositions
5. A conjectural statement that indicates a relationship between two or more variables is a:
   a. principle or law
   b. hypothesis
   c. generalization
   d. taxonomy
   e. theory

ANSWERS TO THE QUIZ—TRUE OR FALSE

1. The answer to statement #1, theory is an expression of someone's personal beliefs, is False. On the contrary, valid theory is founded on

extensive scientific observations and testing commonly over long periods of time. Theory development is based on several steps that range from long-term observations, hypotheses, generalizations, and ultimately valid and reliable theory.
2. The answer to statement #2 is True. A theory does serve the practitioner in many ways including providing the answer for a question at hand or a decision relative to a problem being encountered.
3. The answer to statement #3 is True. Theory is indeed a fact-founded method that provides a basis for effective decision making.
4. The answer to statement #4 is True. Theory is dependent on a series of observations over time. The knowledge gained is analyzed and evaluated at each observational step along the way.
5. The answer to statement #5 is False. Although theory is often confused with other terms such as a taxonomy or axiology, theory is viewed as being research based and scientifically developed and a taxonomy or axiology definitely are not.
6. The answer to statement #6 is False. Philosophy and theory are two separate entities. Philosophy is viewed as being centered on the search for truth and what is real. Theory serves to provide a basis for providing the best solutions to a problem or practice.
7. The answer to statement #7 is False. On the other hand, research in education has been weak at best. History reveals the fact that even when valid research relating to education is revealed, it is ignored rather than being implemented in ongoing practices.
8. The answer to statement #8 is False. Research in education, both locally and externally, has been weak at best. One of the most serious deficiency in education is that of a valid and reliable research base.
9. The answer to statement #9 is False. Although theory has been utilized to some extent in educational practices, it has been overlooked as a viable need in education. Theory that has been developed outside the realm of education has been utilized by practitioners in many instances beneficially.
10. The answer to statement #10 is False. On the contrary, theory does not tell someone how to do something. Rather, theory points out what is likely to happen if certain action is taken.

YOUR SCORE ON THE QUIZ

10–9 correct *****   A star is born
8–7 correct ****   A star is bright
6–5 correct ***   A star of wonder
4–3 correct **   A potential star
2–1 correct *   A distant star

ANSWERS TO THE QUIZ: MULTIPLE CHOICE

The answer to #1 is "c"—an orderly classification according to presumed and natural relationships; #2 is "a"—a term to which a particular meaning has been attached (leadership, morale, loyalty); #3 is "e"—a statement or generalization according to presumed and natural relationships; #4 is "c" efficiency; and #5 is "b" an hypothesis.

KEY CHAPTER IDEAS AND RECOMMENDATIONS

- Chapter 1 has served to underscore the fact that any field that expects to move ahead must have a theoretical framework.
- A practical approach to problem solving falls short of being effective due to its many questions relative to which approach should be used and what is to be done if a selection solution does not work. Just choose another one?
- Theory development is a complex activity that commonly is developed over long periods of time. It is not a simple activity but requires serious observations, analyses, scientific thinking, and decision-making.
- Theory's ultimate benefit is that it provides the basis for making decisions about questions and problems encountered in practice.
- Viable theory is closely related to a fact-founded approach which serves to extend knowledge and understanding on a logical and scientific basis.
- The acceptance of theory is partially troubled by the fact that it is misused by inappropriate examples and faulty definitions.
- Giving thought to what theory is not helps to clarify what it is and differentiates it from other terms such as taxonomy, axiology, philosophy, and others.
- The development of viable theories in education has been inhibited by the absence of ongoing, valid, and reliable research in education.
- The importance of theory in education was initiated in the early 1950s through the 1970s. Yet, a serious commitment to theory in the education profession has not supported its continuation to date.
- Empirical evidence of doctoral dissertation research in educational administration has revealed that little attention has been devoted to providing direction and meaning to the work being performed in school programs.
- Effective theory should serve as a guide for administration action.
- Theory could well serve education by providing a guide for administration action.
- Viable theory is developed over time by the implementation of observing phenomena that has revealed certain results that lead to important inferences and later to directive hypotheses that promote generalizations that are validated and ultimately viewed as valid theories.

- Preparation programs for potential school leaders must improve their program provisions in the areas of research activities, and theory development and applications. Only through this improvement can educational administration reach a high level of performance. Experience alone is not sufficient for meeting the challenges in a world of change. Theory into practice is the recommendation to be pursued.

DISCUSSION QUESTIONS

1. Consider the statement that "theory is the most practical of all things." Write a paragraph or two concerning what this statement is contending.
2. Set forth three specific ways in which theory serves the school administrator.
3. Chapter 1 includes a statement by Andrew Halpin in 1960 that "there does not exist today either in education or industry a single well-developed theory of administration that is worth getting excited about." Is Halpin's statement still true today? Why or why not?
4. How can theory provide a basis for problem analysis in educational administration?
5. How is theory developed? Be specific in your response.
6. Most every model for effective decision-making opens with the gathering of information. Name several important questions that should be asked regarding the steps to be taken in finding and/or gathering information on the question posed.
7. Differentiate between the two terms theory and practice.
8. Explain the statement that "theory does not serve to set forth the ethical paths to follow or attempt to provide the answer to what is good."
9. Take a few minutes to draft a statement of your view or position regarding theory and its importance in educational administration.
10. Take a pro or con stance to the proposition that: Administrator preparation programs are too theoretical. Set forth your opening argument regarding the position that you have taken.

REFERENCES

Barnard, C. I. (1938). *The Functions of the Executive*. Cambridge, MA: Harvard University Press.

Bloom, B.S. (1956). *Taxonomy of Educational Objectives*. Vol. 1: Cognitive Domain. New York: McKay, 20–24.

Cleveland, H. (1980, August). Learning the art of leadership: The worldwide crisis in government demands new approaches. *Twin Cities Magazine*, 27–34.

Dewey, J. (1929). *Sources of Science of Education*. New York: Liveright.
Getzels, J.W., & Guba, F.G. (1957, Winter). Social behavior and the administration process. *School Review*, 65, 423–441.
Herzberg, F., Mausner, B., & Snyderman, B. (1959). *The Motivation to Work*. New York: John Wiley.
Hoy, W. K., & Miskel, C. G. (2001). *Educational Administration: Theory, research and practice* (6th ed.). New York: McGraw-Hill.
Mort, P. R. (1957). *Principles of School Administration*. New York: McGraw-Hill.
Sergiovanni, T. J. (2000). *Moral Leadership: Getting to the Heart of School Improvement*. San Francisco: Jossey-Bass.
Urwick, L., & Gulick, L. (Eds.). (1937). *The Elements of Administration. Papers on the Science of Administration*. New York: Columbia University Institute of Public Administration.

Chapter 2

Educational Theories of the Scientific Management Era and Their Presence in Contemporary Practice

Primary chapter goal: To review selected conceptional educational contributions of the Scientific Management Era and examine their presence in contemporary practices.

The scientific or classical management concept controlled the management of organizations nationally from 1911 to 1921 and has influenced educational practices from that time on. Since the era placed a heavy managerial control over the work place, the managers were commonly referred to as the CEOs of the company. School superintendents were attracted to the CEO title as well and the large majority of them welcomed the entry of scientific management principles into their administrative practices.

We make special note of the fact that many of the concepts set forth during the scientific management era were borrowed from sources outside education for implementation in practice. That is, many theories set forth by individuals for implementation in business and industry were viewed as being appropriate for educational practices as well. For example, theories relative to social issues, job satisfaction, leadership styles, and motivation were not only appropriate for implementation in business and industry but also held implications for educational purposes. Although it is beyond the scope of chapter 2 to consider all concepts that influenced the scientific management era, a large sampling of concepts is discussed.

We make note of the fact that the timing of an individual's contribution to the scientific management era or any other era presents some problems. In some cases, the contributor's work was accomplished during the primary years of the scientific management era, 1911–1921, but was not recorded/ published until much later in history. Some very early work by Max Weber, for example, in the area of social and economic education, was not actually published until much later.

FREDERICK TAYLOR'S SCIENTIFIC MANAGEMENT CONCEPTS

We want to make it clear that the majority of the concepts that dominated the scientific management era were developed by persons outside the field of education. Nevertheless, theories that were focused on business and industry were readily adopted by leaders in education positions. Problems related to job satisfactory, worker motivation, organizational development, human resources, social relations, efficiency, leadership, and others that focused on business and industry were quite applicable to educational administration as well.

This is not to say that educators were not active in the scientific management "revolution." In fact, educators such as Elwood P. Cubberly, James L. McConaughy, Franklin Bobbitt, Elton Mayo, Frank and Lillian Gilbreth, and others became strong supporters of scientific management. Franklin Bobbitt was an educator and faculty member at the University of Chicago and James L. McConaughy was a member of the faculty at Dartmouth University.

The central focus of chapter 2 is vested in the identification of basic concepts that were implemented during the scientific management era, the extent to which these concepts were implemented in education programs of the time, and how these early concepts have been carried forth into contemporary educational practices. The characteristics of concepts implemented in the era under discussion are presented and the extent to which these developments have been retained in today's educational program practices are viewed within the primary purposes of this chapter.

A DESCRIPTION OF THE SCIENTIFIC MANAGEMENT ERA

The *scientific management era*, which was highlighted in the book, *Shop Management*, was authored by Frederick Taylor in 1911. Before that date, organizational development and effective management were unclear and unanswered. Taylor was the first person to explore the concept of the systematic study of management. His basic theme was that managers should study work scientifically to identify the "one best way" to perform a task. Taylor's book set forth the concept that managers were responsible for telling the worker just what to do and how it must be done in the most efficient way.

RATIONALISTIC LEADERSHIP AND SCIENTIFIC MANAGEMENT AS PROMOTED BY FREDERICK TAYLOR

Prior to the beginning of the twentieth century, the question of what it is that managers should do remained unanswered. Before 1900, school administrators, as well as managers in business and industry, were unsure of their leadership responsibilities. Frederick Taylor's principles of rationalistic leadership and scientific management set forth the concept that the art of management was "knowing exactly what you want men to do, and then seeing that they do it in the best and cheapest way."

Taylor's scientific management, commonly referred to as the task system, included the following five primary characteristics:

- All responsibility for the planning, organizing, and designing of work procedures were considered to be under the authority of management.
- The goal of determining the best and cheapest way to do the task was also the manager's responsibility. Such procedures as time and motion strategies were used to determine the most efficient way of doing the job.
- Selection of the best person for the task at hand was another concern of the manager. Selection criteria included such scientific considerations as physical stature of the man and the size of the shovel that would be used for shoveling coal.
- On-the-job training was another leadership role expected of the work supervisor. Incentive pay was an important consideration in the task system.
- The monitoring of worker performance was another manager responsibility. Supervisors were to see that the designed work procedures were in place and that expected results were accomplished.

As a result of Taylor's concepts of management, many practices invaded the business and industrial work places. *Efficiency* became the password for all organizations, and education was no exception. Just as having a highly respected *efficient industrial* organization was prized in the early 1900s, leaders in education were more than pleased to have a highly efficient school operation. In addition, gaining the title of the school district's chief executive officer added needed prestige to the position of school superintendent. Other practices that were brought to the fore in the early years of Taylor's scientific management were job descriptions, incentive pay, line of authority, division of labor, on-the-job training, task procedures, scientific methods, management training, wellness programs, and other practices still witnessed in contemporary educational practices.

Without question, one of the primary contributions of the classical management theory by Taylor was the professionalism of management. This concept influenced professional management nationally and internationally and was quickly endorsed in education. The era brought new practices to the office of the school superintendent. Taylor's influences also brought new program interventions into preparation programs for school leaders. Teacher supervision, personnel practices, organization development, business management, facility planning, and related courses became the core of the administrator training programs. It is difficult to identify a contemporary practice in school administration that is not related to the theoretical concepts that were put into practice during the scientific management era.

Although Frederick Taylor's scientific management era began to wane by the 1920s, primarily due to Mary Parker Follett's new theories on human relations, Taylor's scientific management theories and practices have had long-lasting impacts on the way school administration is practiced today. Taylor's revolutionary concepts served to motivate other individuals to theorize about the concepts of the division of labor, hierarchy of authority, policy and regulations, career orientation, organizational efficiency, position descriptions, and many other practices that are in place in contemporary educational practices.

Give thought to the concept of specialization and the event of the assembly line. Taylor's task concept centered on the arrangement of having each individual becoming an expert on one special step in the production process. The assembly line has been prominent in industry and has led its influence in many of the business and administrative processes in education. For example, the secretarial practices in local schools and central offices commonly are divided among the staff personnel who become specialists in the various dimensions of office duties. Specialization is also changed practices in teaching practices and the offices resulting from the division of labor.

Elementary teachers in the early 1900s most often were teachers of all subjects and related activities. Specialization is now in practice whereby the classroom teacher focuses on one primary academic area of the curriculum and other specialists in music, art, physical education, science, and reading assume the teaching responsibilities. Give thought to the many services that have become specialized practices at the secondary school level. It is not that Frederick Taylor's theoretical contentions were responsible for the foregoing outcomes, but rather that his work served as a foundation and motivation for others to improve and implement the scientific management concept to changes that inevitably become necessary in the world of change.

Taylor's task system was first to require that the manager be the one person who must know what needed to be done and then being certain that the job was done in the most efficient and cheapest way. In short, the management was to know exactly what job responsibilities were to be done and then making certain that those responsibilities were accomplished.

Figure 2.1 Frederick Taylor.

Five primary responsibilities were placed upon each and every manager. First, all organizational development responsibilities were delegated to the shop manager. Secondly, the manager was responsible for determining the best design for accomplishing the job. Thirdly, the manager was responsible for selecting and placing the very best person on each job. Although competency was an important criterion for job placement, physical stature of the worker was considered in relation to the work activities that must be accomplished. Fourthly, the training of the worker for the specific job he or she was to perform was under the supervision of the manager.

For example, the size of the shovel for scooping coal or wheat was a consideration of importance. Efficiency ruled. Lastly, the monitoring of the designed work assignments was of paramount importance. Incentive pay was in place; underachievement was not to be tolerated. Continuation of employment was tied closely to efficient work production.

SCIENTIFIC MANAGEMENT AND EDUCATIONAL PRACTICES

Not only did the concepts of scientific management have great influences on practices of business, industry, and education in the early 1900s, but the concept is witnessed in the management practices of business, industry, and education today. Taylor's task system left many tracks on practices in contemporary management procedures:

- Planning, organizing, and designing of work procedures were considered to be under the authority of the manager. Managers assumed the authority for designing the work tasks and, for the most part, were responsible for controlling the worker's accomplishments. Supervisors were assigned employee roles and, although such roles have expanded over the years, the management assignments remain much the same today. In education, for example, the office staff, teachers, department chairs, assistant principals, principal, and school directors, assistant superintendent, and superintendent still reflect the scientific management plan shown on the organizational chart.
- Efficiency and "best way of doing a job" were specific ingredients of the scientific task system. Efficiency refers to financial as well as human resources and the amount of idle resources as well. Determining the best and cheapest way to do a task/activity was of foremost importance in the task system in the early 1900s. Business managers in school districts today, along with other leaders in the school district, have developed specific procedures for ordering and purchasing school materials and supplies. Low bid procedures and coordinated "bulk" purchasing, as practiced during the early task system, are practiced today in most every school and school system in America.

  Present school facility personnel leaders serve to test the quality of materials to be used in schools and make efforts to choose the highest quality of materials at the lowest bid price.
- The scientific management task system set forth the goal of determining the best person for the task at hand. Is there any question that the procedures are not practiced in the human resources procedures in school district's today? Job descriptions, experience checks, interviews, vitas, references, background checks, and other work evidence are collected for most every potential hire. Special attention is given to the applicant's qualifications/experience for the specific job to be done.
- In the scientific management system, on-the-job training performance was another responsibility of the manager. In some cases, performance pay was awarded and underachievement often led to worker dismissal. Contemporary procedures tend to reflect these early procedures as well.

- Taylor was concerned with *soldiering* by workers on the job. That is, the worker was "looking busy" but in fact was doing little or nothing workwise. The term soldiering was demonstrated by a soldier who was simply marching in place. That is, the soldier completed the steps required in marching but did not move forward. The common command, "In place, march" would result with the feet and legs of the soldiers moving up and down but the soldiers not moving forward.
- In the scientific management system, the monitoring of worker performance was another responsibility of the manager. Today, the school principal is commonly the one individual that assumes this responsibility. Performance pay is common in some schools today as well.

SCIENTIFIC MANAGEMENT AND SCHOOL ADMINISTRATION

Scientific management sets forth improved methods toward the solution of problems that are commonly met in organizational development. There is no question about scientific management's influence on school administration. As previously noted, job descriptions, which set forth the specific duties related to a task, remain in place in both businesses and school districts today. The characteristic of professionalism shown in today's management operations, without question, can be attributed in large part to the classical management system of the early 1900s.

History records the fact that educational leaders readily accepted the ideas from the scientific management era. Most persons would agree that the scientific management era had much to offer practices in education. However, the factor of control was the frontrunner of scientific management and had too much influence on a professional field that focused on wide differences in student learning.

Nevertheless, the new forces that accompanied scientific management controls brought about needed prestige which enabled administrators to gain new status as leaders in the business of education in the nation. Involvement in the new management concepts brought educational personnel into the accepted practices of other "successful" businesses in the school community.

It took the work of many other persons, including Mary Parker Follett, to turn the tide from the total concept of efficiency and manager control to the realization that schools are people and the human element is the "controlling" element of successful programs in human organizations. The human relations era is discussed later in chapter 3.

HENRI FAYOL AND HIS FOURTEEN PRINCIPLES OF MANAGEMENT

How many of the following terms, set forth by Fayol, can be related directly to contemporary practices/concepts in education: division of work, authority, discipline, unity of command, unity of direction, subordination, remuneration, centralization, scalar chain (chain of command), order, equity, stability of tenure, initiative, and esprit de corp. Virtually every one of the foregoing terms are present in practices today. The names of a few of the terms have changed, but the underlying purposes remain in place. For example, unity of direction, as set forth by Fayol, is viewed in the processes of collaboration, cooperation, and group decision-making today. Similarly, Fayol's concept of stability of personnel expressed the importance of retaining personnel. Today, teacher turnover is an ongoing problem for schools.

Taylor's concepts of the division of labor are prevalent in most every facet of the work in modern organizations and education is no exception. The quality of efficiency is facilitated by having the worker use the "hit and miss" approach to the workplace but rather use a scientific approach to determine what the job was to accomplish and what equipment and human behavior were required to meet that goal. In short, efficiency was to be accomplished by analyzing the best way to complete a job requirement with the best use of human effort, worker time, company expense and with full attention given to the matter of worker fatigue.

HENRI FAYOL'S CONTRIBUTIONS TO SCIENTIFIC MANAGEMENT

Personnel considerations were reflected in Fayol's concern for worker/job qualifications. Fayol gave considerable attention to the importance of hiring quality workers who possessed the education aptitude, work experience, and ability to improve within the organization for the purpose of fulfilling the goals and objectives of the organization. From a personnel standpoint, he believed that a worker's attitude toward the job could be determined before being hired. In turn, such candidates could be trained for the job while on the job.

Fayol was born fifteen years before Taylor and was survived him by ten years. His focus was somewhat different in that his principal concern was with management and administration. He was a French engineer and industrialist who held a top management position in a French coal mine company. He wrote as a practical business man reflecting on his long top management career and earned the title of Father of the Traditional School of Management. He received recognition for his ideas rather late in life in that he was in his seventies before his work generally was published and made known.

Fayol's major work, *Administration-Industrielle et Generale-Prevoyance, Organization, Commandement, Coordination, Controle,* was published in 1916 when he was seventy-five years of age. The English version was first issued in the late twenties and later translated in 1949. Fayol left a positive mark on his own country and many other countries; a mark that we still emulate today. He established six groups of activities that exist in organizations: Technical, Commercial, Financial, Security, Accounting, Managerial. The managerial activity focused on the acronym, POCCC or planning, organizing, commanding, coordinating, and controlling.

Fayol saw these five activities as essential regardless of the size of the organization or the complexity of the undertaking. However, their presence within a job varied (e.g., the managerial activity was highest in the in top level management and low or absent in technical and other lower activities). Perhaps his major contribution was his efforts in helping to answer the question, what is management? His five functions of management have tended to stand the test of time and remain of major importance in organizations today, including education.

Taylor is credited by some authorities as the individual most responsible for initiating the early steps for the first industrial departments in the country. His contributions to the early considerations of personnel selection, personnel training, and compensation were forerunners of specialized services in human resources office today. Taylorism was evident in administrative practices in the early 1900s. Accountability, merit pay, and personnel evaluation received much attention in education in these early years. Although the term organizational effectiveness has replaced the earlier term of work efficiency, cost consciousness remains high among the administrative objectives of contemporary administrative practices.

It has been noted that Taylor's managerial system underscored the importance of doing the task in the most efficient way with the lowest cost. In 1992, approximately eighty years later, Decker and others set forth forty ways to cut costs. For example, three cost-cutting recommendations were to (1) perform a cost-comparison study of programs, identify high-cost programs, and develop plans to remedy differences not justified; (2) tighten up on money management techniques; and (3) schedule buying in large lots. Business efficiency, as emphasized by Taylor, has been a primary concern in education historically. Such contemporary practices are witnessed in the various budgeting approaches operating in education.

Incremental budgeting, line-item budgeting, program budgeting, and zero-based budgeting are representative of cost-efficient strategies. In regard to custodial tasks, it is common for school workers to test the quality of cleaning solutions, floor waxes, lighting fixtures, and time and motion results in relation to task completions. It is common to hear about school leaders attempting to complete tasks in the most effective and cost-saving ways by asking personnel for suggestions for efficiency and productivity on a regular basis.

Taylor's primary administrative contributions are witnessed today in the area of business efficiency that has impacted practices in school business practices today. Taylorism was much more far-reaching nationwide, however. In 1913, The *Twelfth Yearbook of the National Society for the Study of Education* (Bobbitt, 1913) emphasized the implications of business efficiency for educational administration. Bobbitt's commitments to scientific management for educational programs are revealed in his following citation from the yearbook:

In any organization, the directive and supervisory members must clearly define the ends toward which the organization strives. They must coordinate the use of these methods on the part of the workers. They must determine what is necessary for the workers and see that each rises to the standard qualifications of the organization. This requires direct or indirect responsibility for the primary training of the worker before service and for keeping up to the standard qualifications during service. Directors and supervisors must keep the workers supplied with detailed instructions as to the work to be done, the standards to be reached, the methods to be employed, and the materials to be employed and the materials to be used. They must supply the workers with the necessary materials and appliances.

They must place incentives before the worker in order to stimulate a desirable effort.

Whatever the nature or purpose of the organization, if it is an effective one, these are always the directive and supervisory tasks (p. 80).

It would be a remiss to overlook Fayol's eight guidelines for the manager who has to command. His contentions tend to lead toward the current practices set forth the human resources programs in modern American schools. The guidelines are as follows:

(1) Gain a thorough knowledge of his personnel: Know what to expect of them and what degree of confidence he can place in them.
(2) Eliminate the incompetent: In order to keep the unit in good running order, the manager must separate any employee who has become incapable of carrying out his or her duties.
(3) Knowledge of agreements binding the business and its employees: Managers must see to it that written and unwritten, spoken and unspoken agreements that arise from the culture in which the firm operates are carried out (Note: sounds much like professional negotiation agreements of today).
(4) Set a good example: One of the best ways for motivating employees is to set a good example of punctuality, courage, and loyalty. Bad example, too, is contagious.
(5) Audit the organization periodically: Every year, in connection with drawing up the annual plan, a scrupulous study of the structure of the organization be made with the assistance of summarized charts.

(6) Arrange for conferences and reports: Conferences, when well-planned and carefully controlled, can accomplish in a tenth of the time that it would take the manager to arrive at the same result. Reports are also important tools. It's the manager's responsibility to know all that goes on either through personal contacts or indirectly if in a large unit.
(7) Do not become engrossed in detail: A manager should always reserve enough time for himself to think through the main issues and exercise overall direction and control. However, not being engaged in detail does not mean that details are disregarded; a manager must be aware of everything but cannot do everything. Tom Koerner, assistant president of Rowman & Littlefield Publishing Company, underscores the skill of giving needed attention to details as one of paramount importance for successful business practices.
(8) Make unity, energy, initiative, and loyalty prevail: The manager does this by brushing aside dual command, ill-defined functions, unmerited re-proofs, and so forth. Developing initiative and allowing responsibility consistent with the employee's positions and capabilities are necessary. By using praise, encouragement, and discretely "showing" instead of acting for employees can transform abilities to first rank.

Fayol expressed the belief that in any case or situation, that there must be principles. There is a management function to be performed and for its performances there must be principles; without principles one is in darkness and chaos. In viewing Fayol's guidelines for leadership in organizations, it seems as though his views could be set forth today in a speech in a modern conference of school leaders. Give thought to a modern textbook on educational administration. We submit that much of its content would parallel Fayol's general guidelines of such a publication.

Fayol's many somewhat "simple" concepts or guidelines for management underscore many of today's administration practices. Fayol noted that, a division of labor must be established; decisions must be made on the basis of facts; a hierarchy of authority must be established; a system of rules and regulations (policies and regulations) is of paramount important; employee selection must be based on competency; and efficiency is viewed as a rationalistic consideration. Such guidelines and concepts permeate our preparation programs in mostly every modern institution of higher education.

Scientific management would be somewhat incomplete without a serious consideration of Fayol's fourteen principles of management. These principles were published originally in 1916 under the title of *Administratim Industrielle et Generale*. Note the accompanying description of each component and consider its presence in the contemporary discussions of business, industry, and educational practices.

Table 2.1

Component	Description
Division of Work	The object of division of work is improved efficiency through reduction of waste, increased output, and a simplification of job training. The division of all tasks into highly specialized jobs and prepare each worker for being a "specialist" in that one task.
Authority	Authority is the right to give orders and the power to extract obedience.
Responsibility	A corollary of authority is the obligation to carry out assigned duties. A subordinate is responsible to only one person.
Discipline	Discipline implies respect for the rules that govern the organization. Clear statements of agreements between the organizational and its employees are necessary and the state of discipline of any group depends on the quality of leadership.
Unity of Command	An employee should receive orders from only one superior. Adherence to this principle avoids breakdown in authority and discipline. This characteristic is universal in most every school district today. Administrators and professional accountable to their constituents; parents, students and other school administrators.
Unity of Direction	Similar activities that are directed toward a singular goal should be grouped together under one manager. Authority and responsibility should flow in a direct line vertically top management to the lowest level.
Subordination of Individual Interests	The interests of individuals and groups within an organization should not take precedence over the interests of the organization as a whole.
Remuneration	Compensation should be fair and satisfactory to both employee and the organization.
Centralization	Managers must retain final responsibility, but they should give subordinates enough authority to do the task successfully.
Scalar Chair	The scalar chain, or order of command, is the chain of superiors ranging from the ultimate authority to the lowest ranks. The exact lines of authority should be clear and followed specifically.
Order	Human and material resources should be coordinated to be in right place at the right time.
Equity	A desire for equity and equality of treatment are aspirations managers should take into account in dealing with employees.
Stability of Personnel	Successful organizations need a stable workforce. Managerial practices should encourage long-term commitment of employees to the organization.
Initiative	Employees should be encouraged to develop and carry out plans for improvement.
Esprit de Corps	Managers should foster and maintain teamwork, team spirit, and a sense of unity and togetherness among employees.

Contemporary recommendations underscore the characteristics of cooperation, collaboration, and group decision-making that serve to bring about positive human relations and understandings. Can you identify any of Fayol's principles which you do not agree? Which principle or principles, if any, might you consider as being outmoded or unreasonable in today's organizations?

MAX WEBER AND HIS EARLY CONTRIBUTIONS TO ADMINISTRATIVE LEADERSHIP

Max Weber's early work in social and economic educational theory was highly influential in that it fostered follow-up work in the area of behavior science. His work originally was written in German in 1910 but later was translated by Henderson and Parsons in 1947. The concepts of hierarchical structure, division of labor, prescribed competency, organizational policy, and administrative regulations were emphasized in Weber's work. Each of these five concepts continues to be practiced in contemporary educational administration. For example, it would be most uncommon not to find a policy and regulation manual in a school district in the United States. Today, policy development commonly is viewed as the most important task of a local school board.

Figure 2.2 Max Weber.

THE CHARACTERISTICS OF ADMINISTRATIVE LEADERSHIP

Administrative leadership is a contemporary topic that is emphasized in mostly every preparation program in higher education. Both master's degrees and doctoral degrees in school administration are programmed in almost every quality university today. Max Weber was one individual who contributed to the topic of executive leadership. Although the topic of organizational relationships has been addressed by many authorities historically, Weber's theoretical contributions added greatly to the topic of executive authority and remain in practice today. We note once again that Weber's work was published first in Germany very near the time that the scientific management era was in its early stages but not published until later in 1947.

Weber identified six needed controls for having a well-maintained organizational machine: (1) A Division of Labor must be established; (2) An impersonal orientation, a machine-like operation must be void of decisions on the basis of emotions, personal judgments, and varying competency; (3) The establishment of a hierarchy of authority to control operations is of utmost importance; (4) An effective system of rules and regulations is of utmost importance; (5) Career orientation that fosters loyalty to the organization is important; and (6) Efficiency is viewed as a rationalistic consideration. Once the foregoing six characteristics are in place, efficiency is maximized.

It seems clear that each of Weber's organizational characteristics are readily identified in the literature and practices of educational administration today. In fact, each characteristic is considered as being essential in the initiation of new industrial, business, and educational organizations. We note that the concepts set forth by one creator are commonly accepted and later extended by authorities that follow. Thus, any effort to determine the exact time of the first initial entry of any one concept is problematic.

THE IMPACT OF EFFICIENCY ON EDUCATIONAL PRACTICES

Many readers will remember the 1950 movie, *Cheaper by the Dozen*, which featured stars Clifton Webb and Myrna Loy. The story has it that when the Gilbreth family were out riding in the car and stopped at a stop sign, someone on the street would say, "Hey, Mister. How come you have so many kids?" Frank Gilbreth would answer, "They are cheaper by the dozen." In reality, Frank and Lillian Gilbreth were both in the engineering field and experts on the topic of efficiency. Both were well acquainted with Frederick Taylor. Their contributions on work efficiency are taken for granted in school practices today. Efficiency isn't just something that personnel in education must consider, it is a principled thing to do.

The term *efficiency* commonly is defined as the ability to avoid wasting materials, energy, efforts, money, and time in doing a task or in reaching a desired objective. On the other hand, the term *effectiveness* refers to the degree to which an activity or action is successful in producing the desired result. If the program, task, or decision results in the intended purpose, it is viewed as being effective. One synonym of the word efficiency is success. The three E's of scientific management are Efficiency, Efficiency, and Efficiency.

Frank Gilbreth, through his time and motion study techniques, would assess the efficiency in a variety of ways. For example, he would assess the efficiency of coal shoveling by determining the time it took to shovel a pile of coal using a number of different sized shovels. He tested the efficiency of brick layers by observing the worker's physical movements, the type of tools utilized and the overall production of each worker. Reported, in one efficiency study, Gilbreth increased the efficiency of brick layers fourfold by observing their physical movements and specific tools that they used.

Figure 2.3 **Frank and Lillian Gilbreth.** *Source*: Engineering and technology history wiki.

36 Chapter 2

Lillian Gilbreth was a highly competent industrial worker and psychologist in her own right. She worked with various companies in making the kitchen in homes more efficient and helped persons with disabilities to accomplish household tasks more effectively. Both Gilbreths received many awards and recognitions for their work. The term, *efficiency*, became the byword for successful organizational operations during the scientific management era. Just as in contemporary times whereby effectiveness is a byword for educational success, the term efficiency was the byword for success in business, industry and in education in the scientific management era.

GANTT CHARTS: ESTABLISHED IN THE EARLY 1900 AND USED COMMONLY TODAY IN EDUCATION

Henry L. Gantt is considered to be one of the most notable contributors to the scientific management era. A Gantt chart is one of the obvious historical carryovers of an early model for use in businesses, industries, and education activities today. A Gantt chart commonly shows the work/job activities required in a job on one axis of the chart and the time considerations are shown on the other axis. Gantt charts center on a variety of concepts set forth in the scientific management era. For example, charts for measuring utilization gaps, time and motion, maintenance assessments, planning and scheduling, cost analysis, idleness expense charts, production assessments, and work incentives were recorded in

Figure 2.4 Henry L. Gantt. *Source*: By John R. Dunlap ed. - Engineering Magazine, Vol 51, 1916,, Public Domain, https://commons.wikimedia.org/w/index.php?curid=38050079

Gantt's charts. It would be difficult to find a business, industry, or school organization that did no use some form of Gantt charts in their program activities.

In modern practice, a program evaluation and review technique (PERT) chart is used to show relationships when multiple tasks need to be performed. Numerous facts can be collected and displayed in line and circle charts that demonstrate the starting and use of time and resources. It is interesting to note, however, that statistics reveal that Gantt charts today are in use more frequently than PERT charts even though both charts have similarities.

Gantt charts commonly are followed by written documents called LOGOS. LOGOS are used today for a wide variety of purposes, including program results and commercial advertising. A LOGO is a graphic mark, emblem, or symbol commonly used by commercial enterprises and sometimes educational organizations to promote instant public recognition. LOGOS are used to illustrate a company's business purposes. The McDonald's Golden Arch is one well-known example. The point here in is the fact that initial concepts, such as Gantt charts, followed over the years, are duplicated/extended, which results in new benefits for society in general.

It is worthy to note that Gantt's contributions to management and to industry received high praise by The American Management Association of Mechanical Engineers. An honor medal was established in Gantt's name to be awarded from time to time to an individual who has made an outstanding contribution in the world for industrial statesmanship. Education is a vital part of the nation's industrial complex. In fact, historically, the nation has named education as one of the primary factors that support the success of a free enterprise system that the nation enjoys. It is of interest to note that the first Gantt charts were devised in the early 1910s to 1915s and the honor medal was awarded some four decades later and the benefits of Gantt charts remain in place today.

Some authorities contend that Gantt's contributions were more in the nature of refinements that fundamental concepts and thus have more applications in practice.

In any case, Gantt's contributions to the scientific management era and to practices in organizations, including education, have been more than just notable. Gantt placed an emphasis on worker and employer relations, worker compensation, worker development, organizational climate, and the concept of service and other organizational characteristics and relationships that are commonly the topics of discussion and practice in human resources administration today.

MUCH MORE ABOUT EFFICIENCY

Some authorities contend that Herington Emerson (1853–1931), an American efficiency engineer and business theorist, may have done more for the topic of efficiency than anyone else. This is high praise for an individual who knew and worked with Taylor. Emerson founded a management consultancy firm in New York City. Emerson's philosophy on the matter of efficiency was revolutionary in that he viewed the matter quite differently than most persons. That is, he laid down the premise that the prime institutions for the attainment of efficiency were not men, materials, money, machines, and methods, but were theories of organization and principles. Inefficiency, according to Emerson, prevails because the type of organization in general use does not lend itself to the application of efficiency principles.

EMERSON'S TWELVE PRINCIPLES OF EFFICIENCY

Emerson's concepts of efficiency, a topic that captured the attention of school administrators during the scientific management era, were not only highly influential during the time of scientific management, but were revolutionary in concept as well. Emerson laid down the premise that the prime institutions for the attainment of efficiency were not men, materials, money, machines, or methods, but were theories of organization and principles and that inefficiency prevails because the type of organization in general use do not lend itself to the application of efficiency principles.

THE TWELVE PRINCIPLES OF EFFICIENCY AS CONTENDED BY EMERSON

Emerson's twelve principles of efficiency were not only timely for the concepts of scientific management but were revolutionary in their expectations

Figure 2.5 Herington Emerson.

of conduct by managers of organizations. It is beyond the scope of chapter 2 to discuss each of the twelve efficiency principles but each is listed in the following section and two of them have been selected for discussion.

The twelve principles of efficiency (Emerson, 1924)

- Clearly Defined Ideals
- Common Sense and Judgment
- Competent Counsel
- Discipline
- The Fair Deal
- Reliable: Immediate and Accurate Records
- Planning and Dispatching
- Standards and Schedules
- Standardizing Conditions
- Standardizing Operations
- Written Standard Practice Instructions
- Efficiency-Reward

Principles #1 and #12 are *Clearly Defined Ideas and Efficiency-Reward.* Emerson contended that managers and workers commonly had different conceptions of what the organization was to do and accomplish. Goals and objectives were not always clear. Communication upward and downward was problematic in that purposes were not clear and just who was to be responsible for determining them was not clear as well. As a result, persons at the lower levels of the organization had to proceed on their own in determining what should be done. Such conceptions were often much different from those in higher levels of authority.

The efficiency principle of "clearly defined ideals" contends that operations from the top to the bottom of the organization must be clear to all concerned. In modern language, manager and workers should "be on the same page." If the thinking regarding the ideals of the organization are not in order, the results are most likely to be unsuccessful and unsatisfactory. Conflicting ideals are common within organizations today, including school systems.

In one visit with an elementary school principal in a large school district, the principal reported that, during the fifteen years of experience in the school district she had never been asked to participate on a school committee or to participate in a meeting that focused on policy development. Principle #1 suggests that a positive use of high level, medium level, and lower level collaboration, cooperation, and creative input be ongoing in developing and maintaining clearly defined ideals. The foregoing example indeed is not a common phenomenon in all school districts. However, it does exist.

Emerson's principle #12, Efficiency-Reward, reportedly, was adopted by nearly 200 companies. The reward was revealed in such activities as changes in standardizing working conditions and tasks, time and motion studies that revealed worker performance, bonus plans which raised workers' wages in accord with greater efficiency, and by producing routing procedures. The two principles discussed can be identified in practice in many contemporary school districts. Principal #1, for example, is an ongoing activity in most every effective school district today.

Collaboration and cooperation are among the most often scheduled topics in professional education conferences and after-school faculty meetings today. Norton's (2020) recent book on education in the future gives major attention to the topic of social science and cooperative learning that looms important in modern educational programs and is projected as being of major importance in future education toward the year 2030.

EXAMPLES OF EFFICIENCY AS SET FORTH DURING THE SCIENTIFIC MANAGEMENT ERA

Previously, Emerson's twelve principles of efficiency were discussed. Such factors as defined ideas, records, planning, and written standards were among the listing. In today's school operations, educational purposes, accurate records/reporting, planning, and written standards are prevalent in all school programs. Questions related to school purposes such as, why do we exist? What do we hope to achieve? and how best can we serve our clients, the student? Are asked by education's personnel as they work to meet the needs and interests of students. The characteristic of planning precedes virtually every educational activity and program before being implemented. Written standards and procedures are set forth in the policy and administrative manuals of virtually every school district in America.

Although the question of education's purposes is debated seriously today, defined ideas or purposes are always the focus of such discussions. Is the goal of education to prepare student for the future or is the purpose to prepare them for successful living today? A publication by Norton (2020) centers on the answer to such questions. Although the matter of drafting the school district's policies and regulations is somewhat problematic today, the early efficiency principle of defined ideas underlies both sides of the argument; the argument being whether or not external agencies should be preparing a local school district's policies or should this responsibility be strictly that of the local school board.

AN EARLY CONCEPT OF DEFINED IDEAS RELATED TO BUSINESS ADMINISTRATION

Ward G. Reeder (1929) set forth a conceptual picture of the business administration of a school system nine decades ago. Several purpose/efficiency principles were set forth by Reeder which seemingly would be quite appropriate for such programming today. For example, the following citation by Reeder sets forth his perspective of the defined purpose of educational/business administration in education (1929):

> It should never be forgotten that the school exists only for the instruction of the pupil. The purpose and the efficacy, therefore, of any part of the school organization must be measured by the extent to which such part contributes to the giving of instruction. So, it is with all school administration; it exists itself; it is only a means, not an end, and must always be a servant to only to facilitate the giving of instruction.

We ask the question, how does the foregoing citation, written in 1929, relates to what might be written in 2020? The carryover of the 1929 concept into today's views of educational purposes is virtually the same. The needs and interests of the pupil continue as the directing purpose of schools and school programming. Who has not heard the statement, the student's learning activities should be determined on the basis of his or her personal interests and needs.

THE CREATIVE EFFICIENCY CONCEPT OF HENRY R. TOWNE

Henry R. Towne, a lesser-known name, perhaps, but a major contributor to the scientific management era was known as one of the most important business celebrities of the twentieth century. He was known for creating a modern system of scientific management that blended into the production of engineering of products with management and economics.

Towne's concept is given the credit for the development of the Towne-Halsey plan which consisted of recording the quickest time that a job has been done and then using this result as a standard. For example, if the worker efficiency exceeded in completing the job in a shorter time, he or she is still paid the same wage on the job and, in addition, is given a premium for having worked faster, consisting of from one-quarter to one-half the difference between the wages earned and the wages originally paid when the job was done on standard time. A great example of efficiency at work!

Towne (2019) stated that "the true function of the engineer should not only be to determine how physical problems may be solved, but also how they should be solved economically" (p. 1). The Towne-Halsey plan serves as an exemplary example of creative development as related to actually attempting to put efficiency and production as a primary concern of organizations. His inventions in the lock business were extraordinary. His inventions of locking equipment made his company a leader of business in the twentieth century. He produced small household locks, bank locks, and night latches and as a result become one of the richest celebrities of his time.

Towne's contributions to modern practices rest in his strong persistence for creativity and for actually searching for ways and means to implant productive efficiency into the work of the organization while rewarding the worker. He led in the research and ultimate development of "new products" and better ways of implementing efficiency in production. Although organizational management has benefited greatly by Town's contributions, education today still is wanting for the serious implementation of creative ongoing research investigations that result in better educational outcomes for pupils. Education in America, during the last several decades, has been invaded by political concepts that have not been seriously tested before implementation. Thus, like Obama Care, modern educational mandates have come and gone.

CONTINUED: ADDITIONAL CONCEPTS SET FORTH IN THE SCIENTIFIC MANAGEMENT ERA

Carl George Lang Barth, a lesser-known contributor to the scientific management era, is viewed by many authorities as having a great deal of influence on the promotion of the concept. Barth was a mathematician, mechanical consulting engineer, and lecturer at Harvard University. His reputation is based primarily on his experience as a foreman of scientific management who approved and popularized the industrial use of compound slide rules.

Manning (2000–2016) set forth a detailed "sketch" of Barth's life in an article, "Carl G. Barth, 1860 to 1939," vol. XIII: p. 114. She underscored Barth's contributions that ran through the whole field of mechanical engineering and machine design that paralleled the scientific management era. Barth's peers viewed him as Frederick Taylor's ablest associate who did more.

Barth's achievements were far too extensive to discuss completely in chapter 2. However, several Barth achievements are noted in the following summary:

Barth had

- an enormous capacity for work;
- rare experiences in the practical applications of math mechanics;
- many recommendations for better working conditions for the laboring class;
- completed important work on cost accounting, premium systems, and wage scales;
- creative ways of thinking and working which made him a capable, inspiring teacher;
- great success in delivering compound slide rules that had multiple uses in the shops;
- demonstrated versatility in construction and making use of slide rules;
- did a vast amount of work on slide rules, the standardization of machine tools, and cost accounting along with many other contributions to the engineering and accounting fields;
- the unanimous agreement of individuals in the field that Barth's work should receive public acclaim.

Since Barth's work centered primarily on the fields of engineering, mathematics, and accounting, it is somewhat difficult to pin-point his contributions to education as a result of his work. Of course, slide rules are among the "instruments" used in the areas of industrial arts, mathematics, and science in most every science/economics/math class in school as well as in mathematics related courses in higher education. His work in the area of cost accounting is reflected in most all of the activities required in school business operations. Of special mention is Barth's ability to apply his knowledge of mathematics toward the solution of problems being encountered in the shop. Such action does serve to support the efforts of contemporary teachers to demonstrate the important use of math in everyday practices in life and in the working world.

A Mid-Chapter Quiz

Directions: Connect each concept in column 1 with the proper authority listed in column 2.

COLUMN 1	COLUMN 2
1. Henry Gantt	A. Editor, Twelfth Yearbook on Business Efficiency'
2. Henri Fayol	B. Father of Scientific Management Era
3. Lillian Gilbreth	C. Set up an early conceptual picture of business administration
4. Frederick Taylor	D. Established twelve principles of efficiency
5. Max Weber	E. Known for the implementation of work progress charts
6. Harrington Emerson	F. Well known for the work on time and motion studies
7. Frank Gilbreth	G. Set forth eight guidelines for the manager to follow
8. Franklin Bobbitt`	H. Increased efficiency in the home and for those with disabilities
9. Elton Mayo	I. Known for research on social and economic education theory
10. Warren G. Reeder	J. Associated with the Hawthorne studies of worker motivation

ANSWERS TO THE QUIZ

The answers to the mid-chapter quiz are as follows: 1-E; 2-G; 3-H; 4-B; 5-I; 6-D; 7-F; 8-A; 9-J; 10-C.

SCIENTIFIC MANAGEMENT STILL ENDURES IN EDUCATION: AN ANALYSIS BY MADUAKOLAM IREH-2016

The focus of chapter 2 has centered on the scientific management era, its primary contributors, and its implications for influencing education historically. Numerous ways in which this era is "revealed" in contemporary practices have been identified throughout the chapter. In each case, the influence of scientific management's impact on education has been of a positive nature. That is, such factors as efficiency have been emphasized as being positive contributions to modern education practices.

However, in 2015, a comprehensive analysis of the scientific management's effects on contemporary education was published. The article was specific in underscoring the various ways in which scientific management concepts are still "invading" education, but not for the best of reasons. In fact, what some view as positive influences of scientific management are viewed as being negative influences that are inhibiting progress and creativity in teaching and learning.

Although not everyone would be able to agree with the author's (Ireh) perspectives, it is only reasonable that his ideas are known and considered. The comprehensiveness of Ireh's paper is beyond the scope of chapter 2, a selection of contentions by the author are set forth in the following section. As the major purpose of this book is to examine the status of major concepts/ theories that have been developed during the scientific management era, several statements of Ireh's views are summarized herein. Permission to use sections of Ireh's paper has been granted.

Several contentions by Ireh are summarized as follows. Ireh's paper consisted of twenty pages including the abstract.

- The paper noted that schools have remained unchanged in America due largely to the accretion of small adjustments in what remains a very traditional enterprise. The problem is deeply rooted in the propagation and adaptation of scientific management with its emphasis on efficiency and control by educators who applied and/or continues to apply it to education to restore order and accountability.
- Taylor's ideas of standardizing tasks to increase efficiency and output parallels the adoption of high stakes standardized testing with the No Child Left Behind Act of 2001.
- According to Bobbitt (1913), scientifically managed education requires that teachers must follow the methods determined by their administrators because they are not capable of determining such methods themselves.
- The application of scientific management to education also affected the relationship of teachers and students to the process of education: it dehumanized their relationship to teaching and students by alienating them from their own creativity and intellectual curiosity.
- Worthy of mentioning here is the fact that scientific management is not the only management strategy from which education has borrowed. However, no other strategy, theory, framework, or principle of management has negatively influenced educational management and efforts to improve schools in America as scientific management did and, to some extent, continues to do so.
- And, as it did between management and employees in the business and industrial sectors, scientific management contributed to adversarial relationships between teachers and school administrators and/or school boards and to the formation of teacher unions.
- The aspect of "scientific control" separates teachers from significant input in ideas about many aspects of schooling. We now know that improved teacher

and student performance result from allowing and encouraging teachers to breathe life of ideas into their profession (Bridwell-Mitchell, 2015).
- Scientific management with its emphasis on control and the "one best way" of doing work has culminated in teachers being at the receiving end of public criticism. For example, persistent blames for the inadequacies of the educational system I America tend to be focused on teachers (Bridwell-Mitchell, 2015).
- At the present time, teaching tasks in many schools are still routinized and segmented according to established curricula. Control for efficiency is enforced through legislative mandates, state-wide standards, administrative rules and policies, and district-wide evaluation processes. Some schools have changed, while others remain unchanged to the accretion of small adjustments in what remains a very traditional enterprise.

In the next chapter 3, the concepts of the human resources era are discussed and their influence on contemporary educational practices is examined. The influence of Mary Parker Follett on the human characteristics of organizations has resulted in naming her as the "mother of the human relations era."

KEY CHAPTER IDEAS AND RECOMMENDATIONS

- The scientific management era of the early 1900s not only impacted the management practices in business and industry at the time, but influenced practices in K–12 schools as well.
- Frederick W. Taylor is viewed as the Father of Scientific Management and gained the favor of numerous other highly qualified scientists in establishing its principles in business and industrial practices nationally.
- The concepts of scientific management were readily accepted by most every educational leader in America. School superintendents were especially intrigued by the fact that they were viewed as CEOs of the school organization.
- Taylor's leading theme for the scientific management concept was "knowing what has to be done and how to do it."
- The impact on education by scientific management concepts has been revolutionary in many respects. Nevertheless, negative views of the concept have been set forth in the statements of some authors historically.
- One of scientific management's primary contributors to the scientific management concept was Henri Fayol who set forth six groups of activities for management termed POCCC: Planning, Organization, Commanding, Coordinating and Controlling.

- Max Weber's focus on the area of behavioral science added new dimensions to the science management concept. The concept centered on social and economic theoretical concepts related to organizational operations.
- Efficiency, Efficiency, and Efficiency were the three E's of scientific management.
- Time and motion studies that focused on job efficiency were headed by Frank and Lillian Gilbreth. Both were highly competent "engineers" in applying scientific management principles to everyday living.
- Gantt charts represented one obvious example of science management's concepts that have contributed to contemporary organizational practices historically.
- The significance of efficiency was further developed by Emerson and his twelve efficiency principles that included clearly defined ideals, planning and dispatching, and written standard practice instructions.
- Other science engineers focused on business administration and its applications in business and the application of mathematics.
- Carl Barth's contributions to scientific management ran through the whole field of mechanical engineering and machine design. He represented one of Taylor's ablest associates.
- An article by Ireh completed in 2016 took a negative view of scientific management's influence on public education in America. Controls by external agencies and a lessening of teacher influence in teaching were among the many topics discussed in this well-researched article. We recommend it to your reading: *Scientific Management Still Endures in Education,* by Maduakolam Ireh, PhD Winston Salem State University, Winston Salem, NC.

DISCUSSION QUESTIONS

1. Set forth three examples of contemporary educational practices that were "in force" during the scientific management era of Frederick Taylor.
2. The term *soldiering* came to the industrial workplace during the scientific management era. Have you witnessed this practice in any form in contemporary school practices? If so, how is soldiering taking place in contemporary organizations. If not, why has the practice of soldiering been curtailed?
3. Henri Fayol set forth his fourteen principles of management over 100 years ago. Briefly review these principles, as set forth in the chapter, and identify those that can be related to contemporary practices in industry and/or educational administration.
4. This individual was viewed as Frederick Taylor's ablest associate. Who was this person and why was he or she so positively considered?

5. Put on the hat of W. G. Reeder, Harington Emerson, or Franklin Bobbitt and tell us, in writing, about your major theories/concepts set forth during the scientific management era.

REFERENCES

Bobbitt, F. (1913). "The Supervision of City Schools. Some General Principles of Management applied to the Problems of City School Systems." In *Twelfth Yearbook of the National Society for the Study of Education, Part 1*. Bloomington, IL: Palala Press.

Bridwell-Mitchell, E. N. (2017, March 17). "Theorizing Teacher Agency and Reform: How Institutionalized Practices Change and Persist." *Sociology of Education, (ASA)* 88, no. 2: 140–159. Thousand Oaks, CA: SAGE Publications.

Emerson, H. (1912). *The Twelve Principles of Efficiency.* New York, NY: Efficiency, Industrial Publisher.

Fayol, H. (1949). *General and Industrial Management.* London: Sir Isaac Pitman and Sons, (Original work published in 1916).

Ireh, M. (2016). *Scientific Management Still Endures in Education.* Winston Salem, NC: Education Department, Anderson Center, Winston Salem University.

Norton, M.S. (2020). *Today is Tomorrow.* Lanham, MD: Rowman and Littlefield.

Reeder, W. G. (1929). *The Business Administration of a School System.* Boston, MA: Ginn and Company.

Taylor, F.W. (2011). *Scientific Management.* New York: Harper & Sons.

Towne, H. R. (2019). "2019 Call Tracking Grid Report." *Biography.* On the web: https://peoplepill.com/; https://peoplepill.com/people/henry-r-towne/.

Weber, M. (2012, March 13). *The Theory of Social and Economic Organization*, edited by A. M. Henderson and T. Parsons. From the work of Weber (1947). New York, NY: The Free Press.

Chapter 3

The Theories and Concepts of the Human Relations Era
Their Influence on Contemporary Practice

Primary chapter goal: To identify the primary theories and concepts developed during the human relations era and examine their presence in contemporary educational practices.

The controls related to education resulting from the impact of scientific management began to wane in the early 1920s. The influence of Mary Parker Follett and her book, *Creative Experience,* published in 1924, was a primary factor in the change of the tide. The concept of "power with" as opposed to "power over" was revolutionary in serving to bring the characteristic of cooperation and human relations into the practices of organizational management. Her concepts were founded on the premise that organizations are people and the use of coordination within organizations rather than coercive control was the coactive power that enriched and advanced "every human soul."

Some authorities contend that Mary Parker Follett could rightly be considered the "Mother of the Human Relations Era" in the same way that Taylor was viewed as the "Father of Scientific Management." Indeed, she was called the Mother of Modern Management. She was an American social worker, management consultant, philosopher, and pioneer in the fields of organizational theory and management. The following selected quotations exemplify Follett's views of management:

"Unity, not uniformity, must be our aim."
"Management is the art of getting things done through people."
"Leadership is not defined by the exercise of power over, but by the capacity to increase the sense of power among those led. The essential work of the leader is to create more leaders."

FOLLETT'S FOUR PRINCIPLES OF COORDINATION

In a recent publication by Norton (2020), *Today is Tomorrow*, it was noted that the concepts of coordination and collaboration are not only highly important for success today but will be of high importance for reaching success in the year 2030 as well. In 1924, Follett set forth four principles of coordination in the workplace:

> "Coordination by direct contact" stressed the importance of horizontal communication as well as vertical communication; (2) "Coordination in the early stages" stressed the importance of gaining input from all levels in order to increase morale and to establish purposeful policy; (3) "Coordination dealt with the concept of relating all factors to one another so that jobs and their interactions could be assessed and evaluated; and (4) Coordination as a continuing process" was based on the idea that decisions should involve "combined knowledge" and "joint responsibility." Authority and responsibility were to be derived from the actual function to be performed, not from the place in the hierarchy.

THE IMPORTANCE OF COORDINATION TODAY AND IN THE FUTURE

The concept of coordination as a necessary factor for successful administration has continued historically. In a recent publication (Norton, 2020), for example, the following statement was reported. More attention has been given to participative decision-making and various concerns relative to group processes. It should be no surprise that the factors of coordination, collaboration, and worldwide communication have loomed as being of paramount importance in contemporary and future educational program practices.

Follett laid the groundwork for organizational behavior. Follett's human relations concepts, with their emphasis on collaboration/communication, made major changes in the way in which organizational effectiveness was to be engaged in practices. As would be expected, not everyone joined in the support of Follett's ideology. After all, the scientific management concept was working effectively in many instances and the managers of them took on considerable authority and prestige. Some persons thought that Follett was too far ahead of the time. We keep in mind that the concept of coordination was first emphasized by Follett nearly 100 years ago, and yet, the concept has been viewed as being of paramount importance for a successful future toward the year of 2030 (Norton, 2020).

ELTON MAYO'S FAMOUS HAWTHORNE EXPERIMENTS REGARDING THE MOTIVES OF THE WORKER?

Money, prestige, promotion, the physical climate, and room lighting; which of these provisions effect job satisfaction to the greatest extent? Perhaps each of the factors has some effect on job satisfaction, but Mayo found that other factors were far more important for bringing about high morale and job satisfaction in his Hawthorne experiments in a plant in Cicero, Illinois in 1927.

Mayo was influenced by the work of Follett and others. He gave special attention to the various conditions of work including the physical atmosphere, social relationships, individual and group behaviors, and the factor of worker morale and satisfaction on the job. Mayo was an Australian and a professor at Harvard University. Due to his central interest in the individual and group behavior in organizations, he has been viewed as the founder of human resources in education. Mayo was noted for being present to observe workers on the job giving special attention to worker behaviors with special attention given to production outcomes.

Figure 3.1 Elton Mayo. *Source*: State Library of South Australia.

Poor working conditions within organizations were of special interest to Mayo and this interest led him and his colleagues to conduct an early research investigation of workers in a textile mill where turnover, low morale, and worker accidents were prevalent. One unit within the plant was witnessing an overwhelming percent of worker turnover. Mayo and his associates introduced such interventions as work breaks and rest pauses, the morale, and the work production within the mill improved. When workers were asked to give their opinions about the work conditions and possible improvements, the overall morale increased additionally. As a result, Mayo came to the conclusion that such interventions were the factors of both human morale and organization productivity.

However, other follow-up observations were to be implemented and the well-known Hawthorne experiments led to new and revolutionary conclusions. In 1927 and 1932, the Hawthorne experiments were conducted in the workplace of Hawthorne Works of Western Electric Company in Cicero, Illinois. Two groups of workers were involved in Mayo's experiment whereby one group was placed in a room where lighting arrangements varied. In the other room, lighting remained unchanged. The result? The production in both rooms increased but no significant difference was determined in the work production between the two groups.

The foregoing results were somewhat puzzling to the researchers and this confusion led them to additional studies. A five-year research activity was put into action whereby investigations took place in a Relay Assembly Room where a small number of female workers was dealing with the assembling of telephone relays. Several interventions, including work breaks, changes to lower work hours, refreshment services, medical attention, and performance salary plans were introduced into the work place. As a result, work production increased with each new intervention that was introduced.

The new interventions were then reduced and even withdrawn. Reportedly, work production increased to its highest level. The interventions were dismissed as being the reason for work production increases. Rather, it was concluded that "what went on within the worker" was the causal factor of positive change. That is, intrinsic factors rather than extrinsic factors were the causes of the positive changes being realized within the work centers. The attention given to the worker and the group and individual feelings of workers' importance were viewed as the reasons for worker and production positive changes.

THE IMPORTANCE OF THE HUMAN FACTOR LEADS THE WAY FOR ORGANIZATIONAL IMPROVEMENT

Other experiments by Mayo, such as the Relay Assembly Room investigations, resulted in additional outcomes that facilitated the implementation of human resources departments in organizations nationally. This phenomenon was termed the *informal organization* sprang from the observations of worker production controls. Mayo's observations made it clear that organizational production was "controlled" by individual and group behaviors on the job. The rate of production, for example, was found to be determined by a variety of worker behaviors.

For example, production was controlled by the informal group, rather than by management, by controlling the rate of production and "soldiering" on the job. Informal relationship outside the job itself came into play as did the practice of rate busting whereby one worker was producing more than expected by the group members. Such influences as social relationships, grapevine communication, and group agreements serve to control production as opposed to control by the supervising company managers. The importance of informal groups within the organization became a primary concern within organizational development.

THE NEEDS OF WORKERS, HUMAN MOTIVATION, AND HUMAN RELATIONS

Today, most authorities view the office/department of human resources as the most important organizational activity. Human relations and worker motivation have been among the most studied topics of researchers and concept developers. The focus on human needs is evidence in a variety of concepts set forth during the human relations era that first developed in the early year of 1921 and has continued to be attended from that year forward. Although psychologists and other behavior scientists tend to differ regarding their views on what and how humans are motivated, surrounding concepts of motivation have continued to evolve. The growing emphasis on maximizing human resources was due primarily to the realization that organizations progress to the extent that they are able to motivate and develop people.

The term *motivation* comes from the Latin word *movere* meaning to move. In general, various motivation concepts can be classified under two major types: content theories and process theories. Content theories are based on the notion that "things" within us generate motivation. These theories assume that (1) drives and needs initiate, channel, and sustain goal-directed behaviors; (2) drives/needs are initiated when a deprivation is felt; (3) the drives/needs are prioritized into higher and lower levels; (4) when a need is fulfilled it no longer is motivating; and (5) all individuals share basically the same prioritization of drives and needs.

Maslow's theory, Alderfer's ERG theory, Herzberg's two-factor theory, Theory Y, and others exemplify the content type of motivation. Process theories suggest that a greater understanding of motivation can be gained by attempting to identify a profile/behavior process that people go through as they seek to achieve goals. Such theories state that the thing that motivate may be different for all people, but the process of initiating, channeling, sustaining, and finally determining behavior is fundamentally common to all persons.

In general, process theory assumes that people: (1) exert effort toward obtaining goal-directed rewards as long as they hold an expectancy that the rewards can be achieved; (2) people seek out solutions for achieving goals through the most effective routes available; and (3) efforts are sustained while goal-directed behavior is achieved or there is a realization that it will be achieved. Examples of process theories include Vroom's expectancy theory, Lawler/Porter Motivation model and other equity theories. Equity theories assume that motivation is part of an exchange process. For example, the character of a job performance is a derivative of the degree of equity or inequity that a worker perceives for himself when compared to others in a similar situation.

Motivation in large measure is determined by what the person views as "giving in order to receive certain outcomes for self." Equity motivation might take a positive or negative posture. For instance, if a person feels under-rewarded, the individual might take steps to work harder or might assume a negative stance by attempting to alter the efforts/production of co-workers, distort his own inputs/outputs, or even leave the work position altogether.

In this section of chapter 3, the motivation theories of Maslow, as related to basic needs, McGregor, as related to plus and minus satisfaction factors, and Herzberg, as related to job satisfaction tend to lead the way. Numerous studies have centered on the concept of these three approaches to human motivation. Not to know the work of Maslow (1954), Herzberg (1959), Skinner (1958), Vroom (1964), and McGregor (1960) is one of the "five great sins" in educational administration.

In Maslow's system, the hierarchy begins with the basic psychological needs as being the most prepotent in the motivation of the organism and extends through a variety of psychological needs as initially less prepotent, but ready to become more prepotent when the psychological needs are satisfied. As the concept has been extended to the problems of motivation, the basic biological motivations are generally found at a sufficient level of satisfaction so that the hierarchy lies within the various psychological and social needs of the individual.

Maslow's concept has led many persons to feel that the worker can never be satisfied with his or her job. How is one to going to solve the dilemma of trying to motivate workers who have a continuously revolving set of needs? That is, is the supervisor going to deal with the ever-evolving set of needs of the several workers that are to be tended? That is, how does the leader use this theory? In the first place, the leader must be on the alert to see that personality and need dispositions of each staff member are being met. Secondly, the leader must plan to handle any conflict between the individual and the system's dimensions, and thirdly, the leader must define the role for all positions with the individuals expected to fulfill these expectations.

The foregoing concepts contend that leaders of personnel programs must be geared and sensitive to the changes that are continually taking place in the needs of employees. This contingency emphasizes the need for special training of supervisors in the understanding of human motivation, the factors underlying it, and the therapeutic skills with which to cope with the concept is most essential for any organizational-relations program.

Figure 3.2 Abraham Harold Maslow. *Source*: http://www.celebriton.com/abraham_maslow/photo/a_photo_of_abraham_maslow

The foregoing details of Maslow's hierarchy concepts, as we have witnessed, are not commonly practiced in contemporary educational settings due primarily to the fact that they are not being included in the preparation programs for future school administrators. Figure 3.3 that follows reveals a model of Maslow's hierarchy. Examine the hierarchy closely and then ask yourself the question, "To what extent are modern school leaders using the hierarchy in their professional development programs for faculty personnel or in school programs for student development?"

Smeltzer (2004) stated that Maslow's hierarchy of needs is indeed used in practice and is a useful organizational framework that can be applied to the various nursing models for assessment of a patient's strengths, limitations, and needs for nursing interventions.

The topic of human motivation is continued in the following section for two primary purposes. First, several motivational concepts were set forth during the human relations era. Second, each of the concepts has been given considerable attention in the literature over the years. B. F. Skinner's (1957) work, *The Behavior of Organisms,* was published over eight decades ago and commonly is introduced in educational classes. Yet, the implementation of Skinner's concept is seldom practiced even though the announced importance of education, based on a student's primary interests and needs, is a common contemporary pronouncement.

The terms behavior modification, drive-reinforcement theory, operant conditioning, and behaviorism all relate generally to the concept that behavior of an individual can be altered through reinforcement of desired actions, the phenomenon which as set forth by Seng (1990). Skinner's initial work advanced

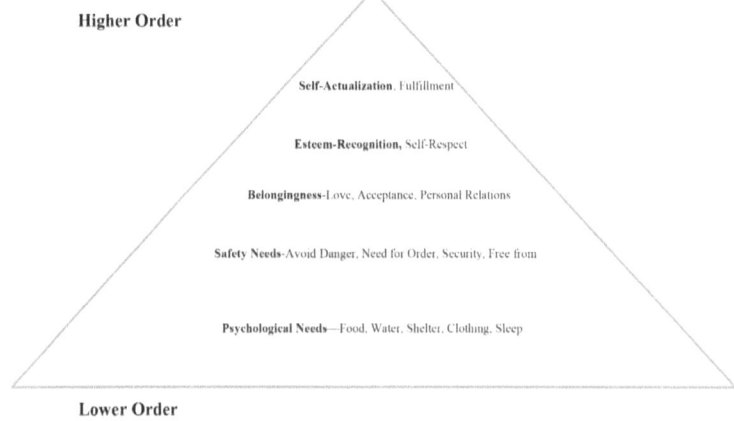

Figure 3.3 Maslow's Hierarchy of Basic Needs. Maslow (1954/1987).

the proposition that an individual's behavior is modified through immediate rewards of favored responses and no response to unfavorable behavior.

MOTIVATION AS A PURSUIT TOWARD ONE'S GOALS

Brayfield and Crockett (1955) and Locke (1968) and others believe that motivation depends upon the individual's pursuit of goals. This form of motivation is referred to commonly as goal-path theory. Forced goals or superimposed goals may gain temporary action, but results are short lived. Simply stated, Locke's basic premise is that an individual's behavior is determined by his or her individual's goals and intensions.

Locke set forth five basic characteristics for employee motivation in his publication, *Toward a Theory of Task Motivation and Incentives* (1968): (1) clarity—a goal must be specific and clear; (2) challenge—an easy or facile goal is demotivating; (3) commitment—your employees have to understand and buy into the goal from the outset; (4) feedback—provide regular feedback throughout the whole process. This helps to keep the goal on track; and (5) task completion—think about realistic time tables and break down the process into subgoals and regular reviews.

Goal difficulty and personal commitment serve to determine the level of effort that will be expended. That is, E (effort) = F D (difficulty) + C (commitment). Difficult goals have a greater effect on performance than generalized goals. Difficult goals result in a higher level of performance than "easy" goals. However, just as long as the goal is accepted by the individual, it tends to be carried out successfully.

THE MOTIVATIONAL CONCEPTS SET FORTH BY HERZBERG: MOTIVATORS AND HYGIENES

Herzberg's (1959) contributions to research and theory on motivation is a challenge to administrators of all fields to provide adequate factors and to call out the motivators which are so important to the nature of work. In his survey of engineers and accountants, he found that events that led to job satisfaction and those that led to job dissatisfaction differed. Job hygienes were viewed as being job achievement, recognition, the work itself, responsibility, and advancement. When these factors were present, job satisfaction was positive. Their absence, however, did not lead to job dissatisfaction, however.

Job dissatisfaction occurred when company policy, administrative action, poor supervision, low salary, poor relationships, and poor working conditions

Table 3.1

Motivators	Hygienes
A. Teachers	A. Teachers
1. Achievement	1. Interpersonal Relations with Students
2. Recognition	2. Interpersonal Relations with Peers
3. Work Itself	3. Company Policy and Administration
4. Responsibility	4. Technical Supervision
5. Salary	5. Job Structure (teacher load, climate)
B. Administrators	B. Administrators
1. Achievement	1. Company Policy and Administration
2. Recognition	2. Interpersonal Relations with Superintendent
3. Advancement	3. Interpersonal Relations with Peers
4. Interpersonal Relations with Subordinates	4. Interpersonal Relations with Subordinates

were in place. The challenge and responsibility of the administrator then is to assess and understand the status of the organization is positive or negative and then work diligently to implement the proper factors if dissatisfaction exists and then implement the factors of motivation in order to bring about job satisfaction. Difficult goals, if accepted, result in higher levels of performance. Goal-path theory has been credited with giving support to the more contemporary concept of MBO.

MOTIVATORS AND HYGIENES FOR TEACHERS AND ADMINISTRATORS

Herzberg's two-factor theory of job satisfaction has been applied for many different professions. For the profession of teachers and administrators, the following motivators and hygienes have been identified (Herzberg, Mausner, and Snyderman, 1959 and Sergiovanni, 1967).

The inclusion of student and teacher motivation concepts are commonly included in preparation programs for teachers and administrators' preparation programs. Not to do so would be viewed as an oversight on the part of the program. However, it is virtually impossible to find a teacher or administrator who is fully aware of the many motivation concepts and also utilizes them in their professional work. We conducted an unscientific survey of a few teachers and administrators and asked them about their utilization of such theories in their daily work activities. Although we often learned that practicing educators used various ways of motivating their faculty or students, we never received a reply that centered on their use of one or more of the popular motivation theories in their practice.

ONE MORE LOOK AT MOTIVATION IN TERMS OF THEORY X AND THEORY Y

Douglas McGregor was a social psychologist who emphasized the importance of human attitudes in supervising workers. His Theory X and Theory Y, set forth in 1960, brought about new thinking for the practicing administrator. According to McGregor, administrators who subscribe to Theory X are guided in their action by generalizations such as the workers are immature, lazy, and self-indulged; they see only the intrinsic aspects of their job and require a highly supervisory form of management.

On the other hand, Theory Y workers are guided in their generalizations much differently. That is, employees are responsible, hardworking, and interested in making contributions to the purposes of the organization. McGregor perceived the manager as a leader who would not be able to please all the workers but should be sensitive to the needs of all of them. Theory Y was considered as the actual potential of all workers. That is, workers do seek opportunities to do their best for the organization as opposed to being laggards that do "soldiering" on the job; that is, they pretend to be working diligently but are actually "marching in place."

CHESTER BARNARD AND HIS "BEST BOOK" FOR EDUCATIONAL ADMINISTRATION

Chester Barnard's book, *The Functions of the Executive* (1939), is viewed by many authorities as the best book ever written in the area of educational administration. His contention that effective organizations must have purposes has been a concept that has carried on historically in educational administration. Without question, Barnard's views on cooperative purposes not only are reflected in every contemporary statement of organization effectiveness but tend to lead the list of qualities/characteristics needed for success in the future as well. The point, purpose continues to be of primary importance in decisions of educational programming.

In the relatively recent publication, *The Principal as Student Advocate* (Norton, Kelly, and Battle, 2012), the authors suggest that the reader deal with the purpose question. "What is our purpose for being here?" "Why does our school exist?" "What do we stand for?" Barnard saw the establishment of a common purpose as an ongoing process, with the repeated adoption of new purposes. He saw the establishment of a common purpose as an ongoing process, with the repeated adoption of new purposes. He emphasized communication as being essential to linking the common purpose of the formal organization with those willing to cooperate in it.

ETZIONI AND THE COMPLIANCE THEORY

Goals and purposes have been discussed previously in the chapter. Etzioni (1975, 1997) stated that the means that one uses to gain commitment to goals and to stimulate activity depends on three conditions: (1) the nature of the goals to be achieved; (2) the kinds of involvement one wishes from those who are to do the work; and (3) the nature of the tasks which defines the task.

Etzioni stated that if the primary goal of the organization is order and the tasks are largely routine, the most efficient means to compliance are largely routine, and the most efficient means to compliance are coercive. The price one pays for this efficiency is that involvement of participants is alienative. If the goal is primarily economic and the tasks are seen as largely instrumental means to this end, then the most efficient means to compliance is utilitarian. In this kind of organization, calculative involvement predominates. That is, involvement centers on material rewards.

If the goals are cultural in nature, the normative methods are needed. Cultural goals and expressive tasks, according to the theory, require moral commitment from those involved. One engages in the organization activities because they are good, can be rationally defended, make sense, and not because one is commanded, paid, or coerced to do so. Schools obviously cannot operate for long periods of time with alienated teachers or students. They can function perhaps on the basis of what's in it for me. This sort of involvement is undesirable. Schools of today are found to be largely cultural and goals are achieved through normative compliance strategies. Herzberg's Theory Y is one example of normative compliance structure.

It seems necessary to note here that the purpose of this book is to examine the primary theories/concepts that have been set forth historically have had influence for educational program practices. The foregoing Theory Y illustrates the difficulty of pinpointing a theory's follow-up, if any, in education. Although the various organizational goals set forth by Etzioni might be somewhat evident in various contemporary settings, identifying the concept as being universal in educational practices is difficult at best.

VROOM'S MOTIVATIONAL MODEL: EXPECTANCY, INSTRUMENTALITY, AND VALENCE

It seems logical that a person will work hard if he or she believes the personal effort will lead to good performance and that good performance, in turn, will result in appropriate rewards. Vroom presented this concept of expectancy theory in his publication, *Work and Motivation,* in 1964 nearly six decades ago. He viewed the central problems of motivation as the explanation of choices made by organisms among different voluntary responses.

His several concepts included *expectancy, instrumentality, and valence.* Expectancy is a belief that a particular act will be followed by a particular outcome. That is, the degree of certainty that a given effort will yield a specified performance level. That is, the perceived attractiveness of the rewards associated with the end results: the degree to which the outcome is desirable or undesirable.

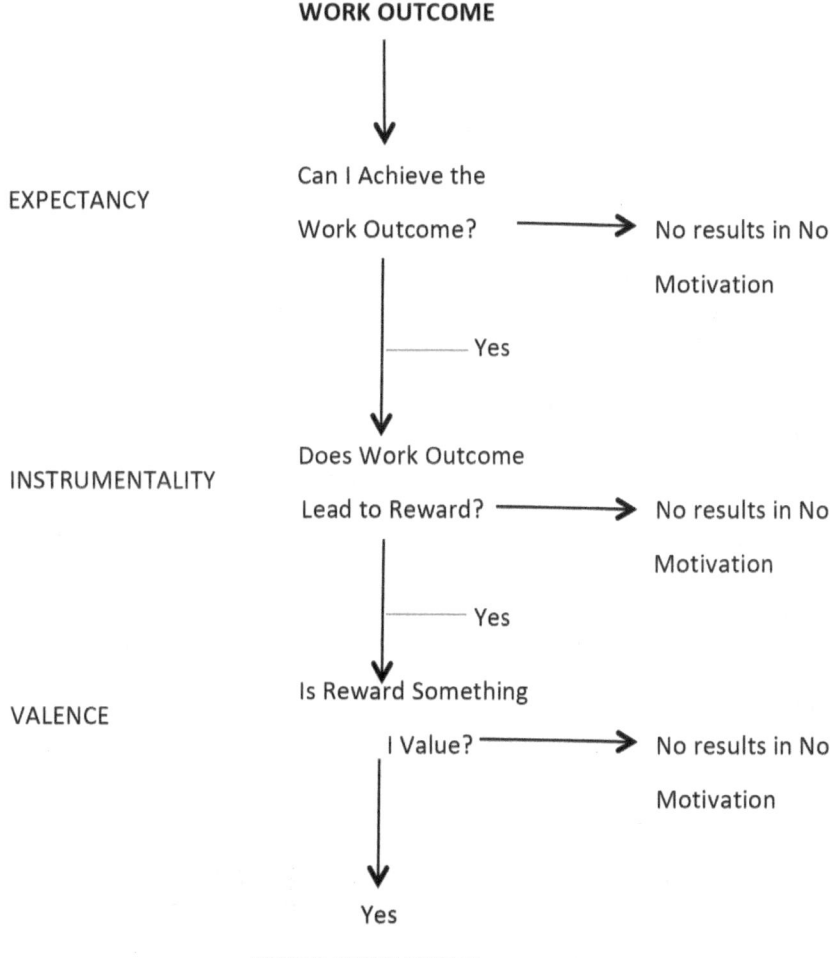

Figure 3.4 Vroom's Expectancy Theory Model. V. H. Vroom (1964). *Source*: Work and Motivation. New York: Wiley.

Instrumentality is the extent to which the person believes an action will lead to desired consequences or present undesirable consequences. Will the reward be forthcoming following an action? This answer depends on the person's perception of the reinforcement contingencies existing in the organization. *Expectancy* is the belief that a particular act will be followed by a particular outcome—that is, the degree of certainty that a given effort will yield a specified performance level. This concept argues that effort and performance depend upon the individual's perceptions of their potential for meeting personal reward outcomes. Expectancy theory suggests that effort, performance, and rewards are inextricably related.

For example, the obtaining of a degree or credential would be "motivational" if the individual was highly motivated toward a career goal that required obtaining such credentials. Expectancy theory supports the belief that employees put forth the required effort and are more productive when they perceive a relationship among effort, performance, and reward. A simplified version of the theory is: M = E × V (motivation equals expectancy × valence).

Consider a worker trying to decide whether to violate a safety rule in carrying out an assignment. If the worker violates the rule, the job can be finished faster which would result in the earning of more money. Violating the rule might have several consequences: being caught might lead to being fired; earning more money is desirable but having an accident or getting fired are most undesirable. Will the worker observe the safety rule or not? Statistical calculations are available that compare outcome valence and expectancy. According to the expectancy theory, the more attractive alternative is to violate the rule.

It is beyond the scope of chapter 3 to detail Vroom's calculation procedures in-depth. However, the basic formula for the calculation is: FM = E € (IV): E expectancy times the cross products summed; that is the response value for each instrumentality item must be multiplied by the response value of the parallel valence item and then all are summed. The procedure here is set forth simply to indicate the in-depth thinking of Vroom in theorizing the concept of motivation. Figure 3.5 additionally illustrates Vroom's theory. Although one could assume that school administrators use various methods for engaging/motivating employees in their work responsibilities, the specific applications of theories such as Vroom's expectancy theory are doubtful.

MOTIVATIONAL THEORY: VROOM'S EXPECTANCY THEORY

Expectancy theory supports the belief that workers put forth the required effort and are more productive when they perceive a relationship among the factors of effort, performance, and reward.

HANLON'S THEOREM 21: ENERGY IS RELEASED IN PROPORTION TO PERCEIVED INVOLVEMENT

Hanlon's Theorem 21 (1938) is significant in that it contends that an individual will act on the basis of task involvement in a positive or a negative direction depending on one's personal ego involvement. That is, the individual will become a member of an organization, patronize a certain enterprise, or might become a grumbling worker but will not be a creative, efficient worker either for or against a cause unless he or she sees a personal ego involvement: what's in it for me!

Figure 3.5 demonstrates the nature of the individual's involvement in a task. The model demonstrates involvement on the basis of task activity and ego participation.

Ego involvement	Task involvement	0 Non-involvement	Task involvement	Ego involvement
	$D^-\ C^-\ B^-\ A^-$		$A^+\ B^+\ C^+\ D^+$	
Participation	Activity		Activity	Participation

Figure 3.5 Hanlon's Theorem 21.

- Right of center, the perception is that of task involvement wherein energy is directed toward compliance rather than resistance. At the left of center, perceived task involvement releases energy but in a negative (grumbling, griping spirit) way.
- Moving further from center in either direction, the perception is one of personal involvement with creative energy released in either direction. Points B, C, D represent increases of personal involvement either positive or negative as the matter comes closer to the individual's personal values/goals.
- The meaning of the theorem is that, as a person perceives himself/herself involved in a situation at the task level, a certain amount of energy will be released and the individual will become active in that direction. As soon as the person perceives ego involvement, he/she will begin to participate in the situation.
- As opportunistic and basic ideals are perceived to be involved in the situation, participation at a high level of creative energy will begin. The

key centers on how the situation is perceived; does the task advance the individual toward personally held goals? If so, energy will be released in the direction of positive involvement. If perceived as detrimental to the personal goals, energy will be released in opposition to the matter at hand.

The point is this: If the organization is to call forth its highest levels of creative energy, it must persuade all members that the situation does in fact involve the organization at levels of personally held goals/ideals held by the membership. It is interesting to note that this contention was set forth by Barnard in 1938.

One might conclude that mandated controls for educational programming have not been successful since such controls tend to focus on the noninvolvement factors described in Hanlon's theorem 21. Virtually every theorem/concept set forth during the human relations era is founded on the positive involvement of the worker in program activities and policy development and implementation.

GOAL-PATH MOTIVATION: A "FIRST COUSIN" OF HANLON'S THEOREM 21

The goal-path motivation concept is credited to Locke (1968) and closely related to Hanlon's theorem 21 set forth thirty years earlier and Brayfield and Crockett's motivation theory of 1955. The goal-path theory of motivation stipulates that motivation depends on the individual's pursuit of important goals. The stronger the personalization of the goal, the more incentive it has for the individual. Forced goals or superimposed ones may gain temporary action, but results are commonly short lived. Simply stated, Lock's basic premise is that an individual's behavior is determined by his/her goals and intentions.

Goal difficulty and personal commitment to attain the level of effort that will have to be expended is formalized as: $E = f(D + C)$ or effort is a function of difficulty and commitment. Specific goals tend to have a greater effect on commitment than generalized goals. Difficult goals result in higher performance levels than "easy" goals as long as the goal is accepted by the individual. Both of these contentions, specific and difficult, were research by Locke. Higher productivity and better performance were found for a variety of workers that included salesmen, office workers, truck drivers, and managers.

What more recent administrative concepts have gained impetus due to goal-path theory? The answers include the more contemporary practices of MBO and competency-based performance. Raia (1974) viewed

MBO as being consistent with the path-goal theory of motivation because MBO is based on the establishment of clearly defined work objectives, progress assessments, a relationship between appraisal and development and compensation, and the element of participation in cooperative goal setting.

Competency-based performance is revealed in modern human resources programs and activities in several ways. For example, the concept has influenced the assessment of administrative effectiveness. The tasks, skills, and indicators of skills of the human resources function are identified and used as the criteria for performance evaluations (Norton, 2008). Performance compensation, although not universal within the educational field, has found a place in many compensation programs nationally.

HUMAN RELATIONS AND LEADERSHIP STYLES

Early studies by Lewin and colleagues in the late 1930s have influenced the concepts of administrative leadership since that time forward. The primary focus of these studies underscored the characteristics of three types of leadership namely authoritarian, democratic, and laissez-faire. The labels of worst, best, or satisfactory were avoided and the emphasis was placed on the efficacy of each kind of leadership. That is, which type of leadership produced the desired results?

Authoritarian leadership was defined as a controlling type of leadership that was similar to the concepts set forth by Taylor in management practices. The leader set the goals that were to be accomplished and oversaw the work to be certain that the goals indeed were achieved. *Democratic* leadership, on the other hand, was characterized by the implementation of cooperative leadership approaches whereby decision-making was much more of a collaborative process. *Laissez-faire was more of a free-rein* approach in that personal initiative was encouraged with few requirements for workers to comply.

What results could be expected with the implementation of each of the three types of leadership? Lewin and others did find that the outcomes of each of the three leadership types were different. Somewhat surprisingly, the autocratic type of leadership did bring about the highest level of work production. However, this result was accompanied by lower levels of worker cooperation and morale and higher levels of worker frustration and personal initiative.

Laissez-faire leadership was found to be accompanied by inferior work production, increased job dissatisfaction, and inferior work quality. The outcomes of democratic leadership brought about a variety of positive human characteristics including superior morale, positive cooperation, group unity, and self-direction. Higher levels of work quality and increased levels of self-direction were positive outcomes as well.

What followed the research studies by Lewin was a revolutionary change in the focus of administrative leadership. In fact, the term democratic leadership was accompanied by democratic schools, democratic supervision, democratic teaching, democratic administration, and democratic practices. Democratic leadership was the focus of best practiced in all organizations and education was no exception. In contemporary educational practices today, democratic principles become visible in the concepts of cooperation, collaboration, self-fulfillment, administrative decision-making, and democratic teacher-student relationships.

Democratic practices in schools more recently have been invaded by external agencies of the state and federal government. Local control indeed has been eroded and administrator self-initiative has been reduced. Legal mandates and requirements must be followed or school funding will not be available. Yet, cooperation, collaboration, and group efforts are being recommended for school program effectiveness today.

As noted by Norton and others (2012), "The first basic ingredient of leadership is a guiding vision. The leader has a clear idea of what he wants to do ... and the strength to persist in the face of setbacks, even failures" (p. 39). The principal's vision is shared with faculty, staff and stakeholders, and they are given the opportunity to further shape it and give it its final collaborative form. Only then will a complete understanding of and commitment to the vision be achieved. The vision becomes the target toward which the strategic movement of the school will aim. Faculty, staff, and stakeholders will say, "This is where we want to go and what we want to become." Once again, the importance of purpose leads the way.

A FOCUS ON SELECTED THEORIES/CONCEPTS AND THEIR INFLUENCE ON CONTEMPORARY PRACTICES

There is no question about the fact that contemporary recommendations for student learning is to have learning that centers on the student's primary interests and needs. This principle is evidenced in the manner in which Jean Piaget's concepts (1952) are being practiced by teachers in school today. Piaget's concepts emphasized the need for the school's curriculum should be programmed according to the child's learning activities that are directly related to the child's present stage of conceptual development. The child's stage of development determines the difficulty of the learning experiences.

In addition, student involvement in the learning activities, interactive group involvement and today in effective school programs the technological software is available so that the pupil can become active as a self-learner. A variety of group activities is necessary for the pupil to gather information on the basis of personal experience. Listening to the teacher, who is voicing information from the front of the classroom, is set aside for the student to engage in self-developed learning. Rote learning is set aside; the factors of personal experience and not being told just what and how to solve a problem or complete a task, are set in place in this way. Children are able to focus on their own interests and personal desires. These activities favor the concepts of Piaget in his book, *Theory of Cognitive Development*, published in 1952.

LOST AND FOUND: VYGOTSKY'S THEORY ON COGNITIVE DEVELOPMENT

Lev Vygotsky's was born in 1896 and died in 1934. However, his work on cognitive development and learning was unknown until much later in 1962 (Farr, 2014). Cognitive theory centers on the concepts that a child's interaction and imaginative play serve a major part in cognitive development in children and their learning. That is, the social interactions that children have help them in positive ways to discover and create meaning from their discovery experiences.

The child may not be able to say word "dog" for example but smiles when the dog comes near. By showing the child pictures of the dog or holding the dog up and repeating the dog's name, Katie, the child begins to make sounds that communicate the name of the dog. The strategy was given the name *scaffolding*. Scaffolding is a procedure in which the child is given help by an adult who shows the child other ways to develop certain skills that he or she cannot do independently.

Vygotsky contended that social speech, private speech, and silent inner speech were three forms of language related to a child's development. When people talk together, this was viewed as social speech. When a child directs speech to himself or herself, this was viewed as private speech. Silent speech is exemplified when private speech tends to lessen to the extent that it becomes increasingly self-regulated.

Farr (2014) contends that "the most important application that an educator can put into place from Vygotsky's theory is his concepts of proximal development and scaffolding. This allows teachers to realize what a child can do if they only had assistance. They can then provide the necessary scaffolding to help the child develop the skill on their own" (p. 3).

THE INFLUENCE OF THE HUMAN RELATIONS ERA: THE ERA ITSELF HAD MAJOR INFLUENCES ON CONTEMPORARY PRACTICES IN EDUCATION

One can find the traces of the scientific management era on contemporary educational practices at both the administrative and the instructional areas of practice. Recent educational standards for K–12 programs were specifically in force during the Obama presidential era and the common core mandates. There is little question that common core "controls" left their impressions on school practices in many school districts. Yet, the "features" of the human relations era are most present in contemporary school practices.

Just the growth of a human resources office in most every school district in America reveals one major reflection of the influence of Parker, McGregor, Vroom, Herzberg, and others that stressed the importance of the human factor in organizational programming.

Many authorities view the human resources function as the most important function in effective organizations today. The contention that schools are people has risen from Follett's human cooperation concepts to a realization that the effectiveness of the human resources within the organization is the foundation for successful program. School programs will improve as the human resources are developed.

A BREAK FOR A MULTIPLE CHOICE QUIZ

1. A school is experiencing problems in the areas of high staff turnover and staff morale. Which theory/concept below might prove to be most helpful as one begins to collect data toward the solution to these problems?
   a. Herzberg's 2-factor theory of human motivation,
   b. Barnard's ideas relative to the primary functions of an organization,
   c. a Gantt chart,
   d. Skinner's reinforcement theory of motivation,
   c. Taylor's incentive concepts related to the task system.

2. The statement "work is as natural as play or rest" relates to:
   a. Mary Parker Follett's theory of coordination,
   2. Fayol's fourteen principles of management,
   c. Mayo's concepts of the informal organization,
   d. Likert's system 4 organization,
   e. McGregor's Theory Y.

3. Mary Parker Follett's conflict resolution concepts centered on the process of:
   a. politics,
   b. coordination,
   c. integration,
   d. quid pro quo,
   e. TQM.

4. Elton Mayo's work found that human motivation depends on the process of:
   a. the payment of adequate monetary incentives,
   b. improvement of the physical facilities in which the employee works,
   c. simply improving the lighting within the workplace,
   d. providing work breaks, decreasing working hours, and providing refreshments,
   e. the Hawthorne effect that was fostered by personal motivation factors as opposed to external factors that were impersonal such as the nature of the worker's site facilities or work breaks.

5. Maslow set forth a hierarchy of basic needs. Which need disposition had to be satisfied, according to Maslow, before the social need could become a major motivator?
   a. esteem needs,
   b. safety need,
   c. self-actualization needs,
   d. self-reliance needs,
   e. none of the above.

6. Motivation theories such as the two-factor theory set forth by Herzberg and others centered on the characteristics of those factors that bring about:
   a. favorable work climates,
   b. factors that served as motivators in job satisfaction,
   c. factors that served as hygienes in job satisfaction,
   d. new and/or purpose facilitators,
   e. motivational constructs.

7. Mary Parker Follett's concept of integration would be applied by a school leader for the purpose of:
   a. resolving conflict between two parties,
   b. gaining control over an individual or group of individuals who are reducing organizational productivity through informal methods,
   c. reducing problems of diversity within the organization,
   d. increasing productivity,
   e. cutting back the red tape within a bureaucracy.

8. Theory X of McGregor's Theory X and Theory Y concept:
   a. views the worker as one with great potential for leadership success,
   b. is based on the plus characteristics for effective organizational development,
   c. views the worker as an individual with little incentive and a negative work attitude,
   d. shows the unknown but potential leadership qualities of the normal worker,
   e. sees the worker as having certain problems but also with high potential.

9. Mary Parker Follett would view the settlement of internal worker apathy as being resolved by:
   a. invoking a process termed integration,
   b. ignoring the problem and letting it resolve itself,
   c. getting the entire staff together and setting forth the "rules" for continued employment in the organization,
   d. allowing the persons involved in the matter to determine the best solution,
   e. invoking a process termed inverse rationalization.

10. The entry of the human relations era served to place a new focus on:
    a. a renewed implementation of management controls and supervision,
    b. the need to redefine the educational practices that were presently in place,
    c. the motivation of the worker through new strategies for compensation,
    d. preparing teachers for the implementation of curricular programs,
    e. viewing organizations as human systems needing a cooperative working climate for program success.

THE ANSWERS TO THE FOREGOING MULTIPLE CHOICE QUIZ

1. The answer to question #1 is "a," Herzberg's two-factor motivation theory. Skinner's reward theory, as well as his no response theory, appears to be less effective in case #1. Improvement is more likely to result if the leader focuses, first of all, on removing the negative factors that are causing the problem (poor interpersonal relations, ineffective technical supervision, negative school policy, etc.). In turn, the implementation of the motivational factors would be in order (opportunities for achievement, recognition for work well done, worker responsibility, etc.).

2. The answer to question #2 is "e," related to McGregor's Theory Y. Theory X leadership views the worker as disliking work and will avoid it if at all possible. The average person lacks ambition, avoids responsibility, and seeks security and economic rewards above all else. Thus, Theory Y is the answer for question #2.
3. The answer to question #3 is "b" coordination. Follett expressed the concept of coordination as opposed to hierarchical controls. Coordination was viewed as facilitation communication, a factor for effective decision-making, gaining positive relationships, and keeping these factors in place within the organization in an ongoing fashion.
4. The answer to question #4 is "e," the characteristic of importance, recognition and well-being as opposed to the nature of the work site facilities and special work arrangements such as breaks and special favors.
5. The answer to question #5 is "b," the safety need. Security and freedom from fear were associated with the safety need. These needs preceded the social needs which included belonging, acceptance, and positive personal relationships.
6. The answers to question #6 are "b" and "c," those factors that being about job satisfaction and dissatisfaction. The interesting and beneficial result of the concept is that those factors that serve to being about job satisfaction are different than those factors that result in job dissatisfaction. That is, if job dissatisfaction is in place within the organization, merely removing those factors does not being about job satisfaction. Rather, factors that bring about job satisfaction must be implemented.
7. The answer to question #7 is "a," resolving conflict between two or more parties. Discussion of the "conflict" at hand is to be addressed through the integration of the parties involved. Communication is sought toward the objective of bringing about understanding and better relationships among the parties involved.
8. The answer to question #8 is "c" a worker with a negative attitude and lack of a high-quality work potential. On the other hand, Theory Y gives an opposite view of the worker. That is, workers do have the ability and the attitude to value work and the ability to do it well.
9. The answer to question #9 is "a," the practice of integration whereby the worker and the supervisor must work together in discussing the matter at hand and determining the best solution together. Integration emphasizes the importance of ongoing communication and mutual respect between and among supervisors and workers and among workers themselves. Only through integration will problems be brought to the floor and resolved through cooperation, coordination, and mutual respect.
10. The answer to question #10 is "e" although other answers do have some value as answers to the question. The emphasis is to be place on the

human factor and its importance for success in any organization. Schools are people and people will be the ultimate determiners of program success. Schools will grow and people develop. This contention is the underlying message of chapter 3. The human relations era brought about the importance of the human factor in organizational effectiveness. People are the schools' most important resource.

KEY CHAPTER IDEAS AND RECOMMENDATIONS

- The concepts of the Human Relations Era that were initiated in the early 1920s served as a change-agent for the future educational practices in mostly every K–12 school in America. The fact that educational program activities were to be planned and implemented with the human element clearly in mind placed the human factor as a first-order requirement in the educational profession.
- The concept of "power over" was changed to "power with" in order to bring the worker into the matters of decision-making and organizational development.
- Contemporary concerns for organizational coordination and collaboration were proposed conceptually nearly 100 years ago. Today, these concepts are projected as being of primary importance for success in the years ahead as well.
- Human motivation and job satisfaction loomed of being highly important in the human relations era. This concept remains highly significant today. The concept that "schools are people" is underscored in organizational development recommendations for school improvement today.
- The human relations era of the early 1920s and decades after was filled with developing concepts on human motivation including job satisfaction, human development, and various means of meeting the interests and psychological needs of human beings.
- Herzberg's two-factor theory placed an emphasis on the positive characteristics of most human beings. Negative characteristics were named but were viewed as X-factors of questionable truth.
- Chester Barnard's book on the Functions of the Executive is viewed even today as one of the most important books ever written in the area of educational administration. Its focus on purpose remains as one of the major considerations in educational/curricular programs today.
- The Human Relations Era itself has had a major impact on the purposes and programs in K–12 schools today. People, student interests and needs, motivation, and engagement of students in a learning culture and self-development are among the many human relations era concepts that remain of importance in school programs today.

DISCUSSION QUESTIONS

1. 1. Explain Mary Parker Follett's statement: "Unity not uniformity must be our aim."
2. The term, soldiering, has been stated in several discussions in the book thus far. What is meant by the term soldiering as conducted in the workplace?
3. The chapter stated that in the year 2012 Norton noted that the basic ingredient of leadership is a guiding vision. Name at least two historical theories that also make this contention.
4. Several motivation theories/concepts were discussed in chapter 3. Select one of these concepts and give several reasons for your personal selection.
5. Pick one contributor to the human relations era as being of primary importance in your opinion. Explain the rationale for your selection. How might you see the concept of your selection in practice in education today?

REFERENCES

Barnard, C. I. (1938). *The Functions of the Executive.* Cambridge, MA: Harvard University Press.

Brayfield, A. H., and Crockett, W. H. (1955). "Employees Attitudes and Employee Performance." *Psychological Bulletin* 55: 416.

Etzioni, A. (2016, March). "Happiness is the Wrong Metric." *Society* 53, no. 3.

Farr, T. (2014, May 13). Vygotsky's Theory of Cognitive Development. *udem: Top Udemy course.* Online Learning Form, San Francisco, CA.

Follett, M. P. (1924). *Creative Experience.* New York: Longmans-Green.

Hanlon, J. M. (1968). *Administration and Education.* Belmont, CA: Wadsworth.

Herzberg, F., Mausner, B., and Snyderman, B. (1959). *The Motivation to Work.* New York: Wiley.

Locke, E. A. (1968). *Toward the Theory of Task Maturation and Incentive.* London, Copenhagen, Berlin, New York & Aukland: Peakon Publishers.

Maslow, A. H. (1954). *Hierarchy of needs* from *Motivation and Personality.* 3rd ed. New York: Harper & Row Publishers.

Mayo, E. (1933). *The Human Problems of an Industrial Civilization.* New York: Macmillan.

McGregor, D. (1960). *The Human Side of Enterprise.* New York: McGraw-Hill.

Norton, M. S. (2008). *Human Resources Administration for Educational Leaders.* Los Angeles, CA: SAGE.

Norton, M. S. (2020). *Today is Tomorrow.* Lanham, MD: Roman & Littlefield.

Norton, M. S., Kelly, L. K., and Battle, A. R. (2012). *The Principal as Student Advocate: A Guide for doing What's Best for all Students.* Lanham, MD: Rowman & Littlefield.

Piaget, J. (1952). *The Origins of Intelligence in Children.* New York: International Universities Press.

Sergiovanni, T. J. (1967). "Factors which Affect Satisfaction and Dissatisfaction of Teachers." *Journal of Educational Administration* 5, no. 1:, 66–82.

Skinner, B. F. (1957). "The Experimental Analysis of Behavior." *Am. Scientist* 45, no. 4.

Chapter 4

Postmodernism

Behavioral Science and the Reconstructionist Movement

Primary chapter goal: To present selected theories/concepts that followed the Human Relations Era with emphasis on the practices of administrative leadership and organizational climate/culture in educational administration. In turn, consideration is given to the extent to which various theories/concepts set forth during this era have found their way into contemporary practices especially in education.

The focus on schools as social systems placed an emphasis on characteristics termed the *nomothetic* and the *idiographic* dimensions of organizations. Successful organizations must do more than just implement the governance structure of management. Effective administration must include the important characteristics of the human dimension or the personality of the system as well. It is contended that the interaction between these two dimensions ultimately determine the behavioral outcomes.

The Postmodernism Era and the reconstruction movement placed primary emphasis on the topics of leadership and the development of a learning culture within the school's environments. The contributions during this time in education's history are far too numerous to present in one chapter. In fact, at the outset of preparing chapter 4, we readily identified more than twenty contributors to the concepts and theories established during the 1960s through the year of 2020.

Authorities and thinkers such as P. Bredeson, P. Senge, G. Bogue, C. Hodgkinson, B. Bleedorn, M. Fullan, V. Cunningham, D. Duke, R. Gregorc, G. Morgan, L. Beck, Etzioni, J. Getzels, E. Guba, J. Burns, G. Anderson, A. Magoon, T. Greenfield, T. Duke, W. Ouchi, W., Foster, T. Sergiovanni, J. Hanlon, and H. Boettinger are a few among the many contributors to this era of educational history. However, the scope of chapter 4 does not permit a discussion of all of the great thinkers of the time.

Theoretical concepts most often tend to bring new innovative thinking for organizational practices and some do remain on the tables of practice over time. In other cases, the "successful" ideas within the theory are put into practice, but other ideas within the theory tend to fall through the cracks of changing times and just fade away.

We note that in a few instances a theory/concept remains in practice over the years. The modeling of Gantt charts is one example whereby the original idea was not only immediately put into practice upon its development, but also has been widely extended in contemporary practices over the years since their first development by Gantt around the turn of the nineteenth century. We do make note, however, that the basic principle of a Gantt chart was credited to Karol Adamiecki who set forth the concept in 1896 over 100 years ago.

THE GREAT INFLUENCE OF THE SOCIAL SYSTEMS MODEL OF 1957

Getzels and Guba (1957) set forth the early concept that organizations consists of two dimensions, the structural and the human, that are always interacting to determine the outcomes of the system's social behavior. The social system concept considers both the goals and purposes of an organization and the distinct personalities of the individuals within the system. The structural dimension was named the *nomothetic dimension* and the human dimension was termed the *idiographic dimension*. This social system model tended to dominate the discussions in administration preparation programs and professional professor/administrator conferences from 1957 through the behavior science era historically.

The topics of administrative leadership, school climate/culture, systems theory, the learning organization, administrative competencies, and the promotion of effective collaboration were often highlighted in publications and professional conferences during this era, but the primary topics of discussion were leadership, leadership, and leadership. Thus, the theories/concepts of leadership also dominate the discussion in chapter 4. The responsibilities of the leader relative to the fostering of a learning culture in the school, creating a purposeful vision for the school, implementing an effective school climate, promoting the development of effective human resources, leadership for curriculum development, and the concepts of leadership for fostering student achievement are included in the chapter's discussions.

SYSTEMS THEORY: STRUCTURE AND RELATIONSHIPS

Jacob Getzels and Egon Guba, leaders in the development of the social systems framework, conducted extensive studies of Airforce school instructors. Based on their research, they proposed that behavior within the social system was affected by two interacting elements, the institutional and the individual. The institutional element in this system is viewed as the "roles" which represent positions, expectations, changes, and relationships. These aspects compose what is referred to as the nomothetic dimension. The individual element, which is defined in terms of personality and internal motivation, is referred to as the ideographic dimension.

The ideographic dimension is the interaction between the roles in the system and the personality of the individuals which determine the resulting behavior. The work of Getzels and Guba served to bring attention to the essential management skill of matching employees with the most appropriate job possible. Figure 4.1 represents a simplified model of a social system whereby observed behavior results from a combination of institutional roles, expected behaviors and individual worker personalities and their needs disposition.

The concepts set forth by the social system's model are significant in their emphasis on administrative matters that must consider both the structural and the human factors in decision-making. Although the Getzels/Guba model does not provide specific answers for administrators or teachers to apply in practice, the model points attention to giving thought to the management aspects of a matter and considering the dispositional needs of individuals in the situation at hand. Empirical studies have used the concept of the model on many occasions. Studies related to human resources administration, organizational conflict, school climate, leadership styles, and organizational culture have benefited by the questions that the concept provides relative to their impact on the organization and its people.

ATTENTION! A LIGHT BULB EXPERIENCE

The contents of this book and the theories set forth in this chapter are based on the work of many persons in many different professions. The concept of the school as a social organization has been viewed as being of foremost importance during the postmodern reconstrucitonalist era in educational administration. The concept has permeated the preparation program of most every administration preparation program in America and remains as the leading conceptual idea for organizational development. Yet, even the

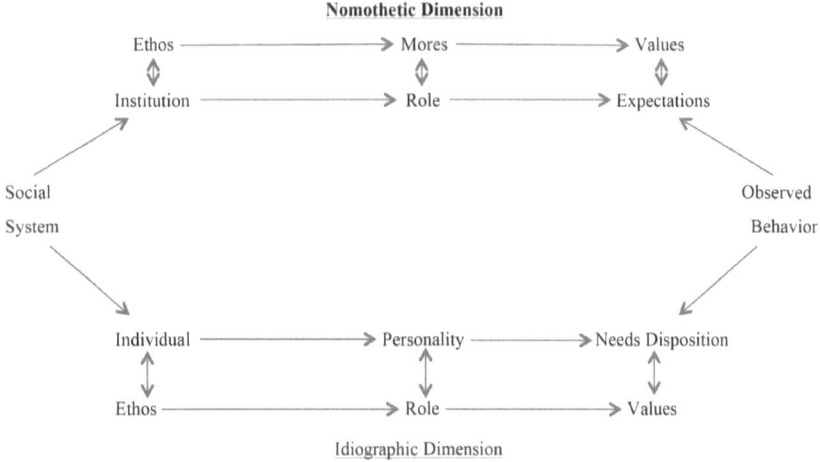

Figure 4.1 Social System Model (Getzels & Guba, 1957).

concept of education as a social system has received criticism by scholars, and it is our opinion that this view should be noted by educators who teach and administrate in our schools and instruct in our educational preparation program nationally.

In doing so, we cite the work of T. Barr Greenfield (1974, July) and his insightful presentation in Boston, England on the topic of *Theory in the Study of Organizations and Administrative Structures: A New Perspective.* The work is a paper presented to the Annual Meeting of the International Programs on Educational Administration. The full paper is available for reading on the web. We present a brief statement within the paper that explains its contentions and objections to many theories promoted and fostered in educational programs nationally. We are not endorsing the concept set forth by Gregorc, rather are presenting it in fairness for knowing about opposing views of social systems theories pursued in-depth during the postmodern era of education.

THEORIES AND CONCEPTS FOR THE FIELD OF ADMINISTRATIVE LEADERSHIP

Which of the following terms are familiar to you: contingency leadership, transactional leadership, aesthetic leadership, heterarchical leadership, exploitive authoritative leadership, transformational leadership, contingency leadership, and the LBDQ? Each of these forms of leadership is most likely to be operating in some school systems nationally. Most of these leadership concepts were set forth during the postmodern era. Each style is discussed briefly in the following section. However, it is virtually impossible to identify any one leadership concept that dominates the behavior of school leaders. Keep in mind that change is ongoing in contemporary organizational practices and then consider the concept of contingency leadership and whether or not it seems to be in practice in contemporary school systems.

Contingency leadership is based on the belief that the degree of required differentiation in managerial and organizational leadership varies according to the nature of the system and its environment. That is, the type of leadership required is contingent upon the demands of the environment in which one is dealing. The key concept here is that there is no one best way of organizing and the most effective kind of leadership is determined by the environment that exists. Thus, the leadership provided by a school principal would differ considerably from the type of leadership required in a different environment.

Transactional leadership commonly is viewed as a balance between nomothetic and idiographic leadership styles. Transactional leadership is based on providing monetary or psychic income rewards in exchange for employee services. The wants and needs of the worker are determined by the leader and he or she provides these interests for members in turn for such organizational needs as task completion, loyalty, cooperative effort, and commitment to organizational objectives (Norton, 2012). It has been known that a school principal might be "unsuccessful" in one elementary school within a school district, but quite successful in another school in the same district. This result tends to support the concepts that underscore contingency leadership.

TRANSACTIONAL LEADERSHIP AND CONTEMPORARY PRACTICES

It has been noted that transactional leadership is contingent upon the performance of the worker. It is viewed commonly today whereby the leader focuses on specific tasks and then uses rewards to motivate the workers to achieve the desired outcomes. That is, when employees are successful they are rewarded and when they are not successful they are reprimanded in some manner or in serious cases are released.

One contemporary application of transactional leadership is revealed in sports' activities. Activity teams rely heavily on transformational leadership. When the player performs successfully relative to expectations, their future is rewarded by added playing time and special honors. At the professional level, rewards are given by way of long-term and highly compensated contracts. When unsuccessful, they are reprimanded or released. Transactional coaches tell players what to do and show them how to do it.

A SUMMARY OF LEADERSHIP TYPES IN PRACTICE

Administrative leadership historically has been viewed primarily as being a science. Some authorities have viewed leadership as an art. The easy response to a question about what leadership really is, is that it is both. Grady Bogue (1985) states that leadership is an art. He contends that leadership necessitates the insertion of values, feeling, judgments, ethics, and other personal qualities and therefore is indeed an art. Hodgkinson (1978) tends to agree with this point of view. In his opinion, administration is philosophy in action and that an organization can neither have "consciousness" nor a "will." Leadership constitutes the giving of considerable morality and responsibility. It is oriented philosophically since it focuses on exercising truth. Such considerations are artistic in nature and are not administrative management concepts. Thus, *aesthetic leadership* is indeed in practice.

D. L. Duke (1986) is credited for extending aesthetic approaches to the study of leadership. He believed that leadership, as commonly viewed as control or influence, was limited. Rather, leadership should be viewed as it reflects the structures of the meaning of the perceiver and the culture of the times. Thus, aesthetic leadership, according to Duke, has several important properties including direction, engagement, fit, originality, the artistry of the leadership, dramatics, design, and orchestration. Dramatics, for example, visualize leadership in the realm of ritual, ceremony, and dramatic performance. Engagement is characterized by the fact that where there are people, there are thoughts, and aspirations (Duke, 1986).

In systems where *heterarchical leadership* exists, there is a minimum of controlled requirements. Rather, flexibility, self-directed and diversified activities are in place. The conditions that exist at the time determine the kind of leadership that will be dominant. *Exploitive authoritative* leadership, on the other hand, is compared to the Theory X type of management whereby threats are used as "motivational" tactics and communication comes from the top-down. The leader and subordinates do not share the same beliefs relative to purposes and strategies for their accomplishments.

Transformational leadership is viewed as administrative actions that center on superordinate goals that go beyond the interests of either the leader or the workers, but do receive the commitment of both parties. Such leadership is termed transformational because it is said to make followers into leaders and leaders into moral agents (Burns, 1978). Transformational leaders call upon employees to work at the top of their abilities to accomplish goals that can be achieved only if each worker gives his or her all to the established vision.

ATTEMPTS TO ASSESS THE VARIOUS LEADERSHIP STYLES

The Leadership Behavior Description Questionnaire (LBDQ) is not a leadership style, but rather an instrument for determining the type of leadership being demonstrated by an individual. One such questionnaire was initiated early by Ralph Stogdill (1945). Early studies of leadership at Ohio State University led to the involvement of several individuals in developing the LBDQ which has been used in hundreds of studies of leadership in organizations nationally. Andrew Halpin and a number of other highly qualified professors served to complete this instrument that included the qualifications of leaders in regard to their relationship qualities (initiating structure) and their behavior relative to friendship, mutual trust, respect, and warmth between himself and members of the staff (consideration).

The study, which included fifty superintendents in the state of Ohio, resulted in four types of leaders; type 1, those who scored above the mean for consideration and above the mean for initiating structure; type 2, those who scored low on consideration and high on initiating structure; type 3, those who scored low on consideration and high on initiating structure, and type 4, those who scored high on consideration and low on initiating structure. In the end, the conclusion was reached that the effective leader was identified as one who scores high on both dimensions of initiating structure and consideration. This finding could not serve as a big surprise. However, Halpin's early work did motivate others to study the types of leadership additionally and one of these authorities was Rensis Likert.

RENSIS LIKERT'S FOUR-STYLE LEADERSHIP CONCEPTS

Reportedly, Likert (1979) spent over thirty years studying the differences between effective and ineffective organizations. The result was his development of a management system that included four different leadership styles. Likert's termed the systems 1, 2, 3, and 4. System 1, *Exploitive Authoritative,* reflected the similar characteristics of McGregor's Theory X. Controls and the use of threats were used to "motivate" the worker. Purpose differences between the supervisor and the worker were inhibiting factors within the system.

System 2 was termed the *Benevolent Authoritative system*. This system featured the provision of rewards for fostering worker motivation. Some persons referred to this leadership style as a "carrot stick" approach to motivation. Input by subordinates is neglected; workers' input is overlooked. System 3, *Consultative* leadership does include some involvement in the decision-making process in regard to their own specific work responsibilities. System 4, *Participative Group* leadership, actually solicits the involvement of the workers. Communication is practiced as a two-way process; talents are recognized and put into practice toward the realization of system goals and objectives. McGregor's Type Y leadership is similar to Likert's System 4.

As an interesting side note, we point out that Likert's name is pronounced *Lickert* and not *Likert* as mispronounced by most persons. We verified this fact while researching the background of this authority (i.e., Lick-ert and not Like-ert).

A LOOK AT SYSTEM 4-T: THE BEST OF THE BEST

System 4-T is viewed by Likert as the best of the best. Its plus features include the high knowledge skills of the leader relative to technical issues and the encouragement of the employee group to become involved in the resolution of the problems at hand. High-level production is identified with 4-T systems, which are fostered by the cooperative relationships that are present in the organization. Fewer problems seem to occur in this leadership style but are cooperatively resolved when such problems do occur. Options for problem resolution commonly are offered by the leader as recommendations as opposed to requirements.

In visitations to various schools and school systems, differences in perceived leadership varied widely. On one occasion, the elementary school principal indicated that the central school district leaders had not contacted her relative to policies or procedures in the fifteen years that she had been a principal in the school system. In another situation, the school had an official site-based system that was "dominated" by the school principal. Parent, teacher, pupil, and staff members of the council referred to their role as being "pons" of the school principal.

In another new high school in the Midwest, the popular school principal resigned to assume a role with a university in another state. The individual, who replaced him, had been named one of the outstanding students in the administration program of a highly regarded university in the Midwest. The new principal lasted as leader for the school for one year only. His attempt to implement a new curricular program within the school was viewed as his downfall.

We understand that the following examples of problematic leadership are both unscientific and single examples as well. The examples were to serve the purpose of trying to determine the style of leadership that is most important for an organization. The concept of changing one's leadership style to meet the school situation at hand. The ability to change one's leadership style appears to be a positive skill but remains controversial. The school conditions that exist will serve to determine the type of leadership that will be successful.

PRINCIPAL TURNOVER: SO WHAT?

Consider the following statistics relative to teacher and administrator turnover in school systems in the nation. Consider the entry of 100 new teachers in a large school system. On average, 20 percent of this group of teachers will leave that school system after only the first year. After five years, 50 percent of the entry group will have left the school system. Statistics relating to school principal turnover is also revealing. On an annual basis, 22 percent of the nation's school principals will leave their present position. No information is readily available to determine the new placements of these outgoing administrators. Give thought to the matters of program stability and the likely effect of such turnover relative to the quality of school performance. What effects might result in the changes of leadership that obviously take place in this ongoing turnover?

FIEDLER AND CHEMERS'S CONTINGENCY LEADERSHIP MODEL

The discussion of leadership is closed by a discussion of Fiedler and Chemers's interesting model of contingency leadership. The interest rests in the way the model shows the eight possible combinations of leadership and relating membership relations, task structure, and position power and their favorableness for each combination. For example, consider a situation when leader-member relations were good, the task was structured, and the power of the leader was strong. Theoretically, what would the quality of favorableness between the members and the leader? The answer to this question is set forth in table 4.1 that follows.

The "controversy" continues relative to whether or not one can change their leadership style to meet the requirements of the situation at hand. There are several different leadership concepts that answer "yes" to that question. Perhaps you might be able to answer the question for yourself especially if you have had the opportunity to work in differently structured positions/

Table 4.1 Contingency Leadership Model

Favorableness of the Situation	Leader-Member Octant	Task Relations	Leader Position Structure	Power
Favorable	1	Good	Structured	Strong
	2	Good	Structured	Weak
	3	Good	Unstructured	Strong
	4	Good	Unstructured	Weak
	5	Poor	Structured	Strong
Moderate	6	Poor	Structured	Weak
Unfavorable	7	Poor	Unstructured	Strong
	8	Poor	Unstructured	Weak

Source: *Leadership and Effective Management*. F.E. Fiedler, & M.M. Chemers, 1974, Glendale, IL: Scott Foresman & Company. Reprinted by permission.

systems. In any case, the foregoing discussion of leadership gives one the opportunity to assess and evaluate the implication of leadership and environment additionally in life experiences.

In the following section, postmodernism comes into play. This concept views administration as being highly complex, unpredictable, unstable, and uncertain. The term *systems theory* comes to life.

ETZIONI'S COMPLIANCE THEORY: STIMULATION TOWARD COMMITMENT

Commitment to the school's purposes and goals is stressed in most every discussion of effective organizational practices. Etzioni (1975, 1997) is one authority that focused on this concern. According to Etzioni, the means that must be implemented to foster worker activity toward stated goals is achieved by the implementation of three specific conditions: (1) first and foremost, the nature of the goals to be achieved is of importance; (2) secondly, the nature of the involvement that the leader wishes from the worker, the person to do the work, comes into consideration; and (3) thirdly, the nature of the task to be accomplished comes into play.

Etzioni notes that if the primary goal of the organization is *order* and tasks are primarily routine in nature, the most efficient means to compliance are coercive. If this condition exists, involvement of participants is alienative meaning unfriendly or withdrawn. If the goal is based on economics and the tasks are viewed as being instrumental to that end, then the most efficient means to compliance, according to Etzioni, is *utilitarian*.

That is, calculative involvement tends to dominate. This result is due primarily to the fact that the individual's involvement is linked largely to what one believes the participation will bring in rewards.

If the goals of the organization are cultural in nature, then normative methods are needed. According to Etzioni, cultural organizations require more moral commitment from those persons involved. That is, one engages in the organization's activities because they are "good" can be rationally defended and make sense to them. The individual engages in the activities, not because they are commended, paid or coerced to do so, but because they are "good" for their perspective.

Etzoni was called the "guru" of the communication movement. He was noted for his views on the importance of having a balance between individual rights and social responsibility and also between autonomy and order. Lunenburn (2012) noted that schools tend to be normative organizationally. That is, oppressive use of coercive and utilitarian power with teachers can result in a dysfunctional system.

Normative power uses the allocation of intrinsic rewards, such as interesting work, identification of goals, and making a contribution to society. The leaders' power in the foregoing case rests on the ability to manipulate rewards, allocate esteem and prestige symbols, administer rituals, and influence the distribution of acceptance and power response in the organization.

Today, schools are much concerned with the ways in which students, teachers, and others are involved in the work of the schools. Dissatisfaction among staff is too problematic to risk. Three basic relationships between organizational types and goal types are noted:

(1) Organizations with similar compliance structures have similar goals; (2) Conversely, organizations with similar goals have similar compliance structures; and (3) Three effective combinations tend to exist: coercive/order, utilitarian/economic, and normative/culture. McGregor's Theory Y, previously discussed, is an example of normative compliance structures.

Question? Are you able to identify the type of compliance structure that is in place in your school system or one for which you are most familiar?

THE FIFTH DIMENSION: PETER SENG'S FOCUS ON THE LEARNING ORGANIZATION

Peter Seng's work on the learning organization encouraged many other authorities to give serious thought to the development of a learning culture in K–12 schools in America. His theoretical concepts are important due primarily to the fact that leadership is tied closely to three types of learning within an organization. For example, the *local line leader* assumes the responsibility for innovating new learning strategies that will lead to learning improvement. Changes within the system that serve to improve the learning culture for students is a first priority.

86　　　　　　　　　　　　　　　*Chapter 4*

Executive leaders, on the other hand, serve by giving needed support to line leaders. That is, these leaders establish infrastructures that facilitate organizational behaviors that are essential for fostering a learning culture within the system. *Heterarchical leadership* is a supportive element that facilitates initiative, self-organization, and flexibility within the organization. In the situation where hierarchical leadership is operating, controlled specifications are minimally expressed and substantial rationality is practiced.

That is, the individual worker decides what is best for meeting the needs of the task at hand. Thus, leadership becomes a broader concept and the characteristics of involvement, collaboration, and cooperation are directed toward the accomplishment of stated system goals and objectives. Give special attention to the how each of the five dimensions for fostering a learning culture in a system is thoughtfully developed.

In Seng's fifth dimension work (1990), he emphasizes the five concepts or leverage points in a system: (1) systems thinking; (2) personal mastery; (3) mental models; (4) building a shared vision; and (5) team learning. A conceptual framework is of primary importance for gaining an understanding of how change in the leverage points within the system has changed things effectively over the years. The clarification of things of most importance serves to personalize one's vision and ability to focus energy on those things that really matter. In turn, the individual becomes more able to develop mental models that can be seriously scrutinized.

Such scrutiny brings the mental models to the surface and serves toward the development of a meaningful "shared vision" of the future. Genuine commitment to a vision of the future, rather than mere compliance, becomes possible. Thinking together, fostering team dialogue, collaboration, and team building lead to what is viewed as team learning. As noted by Seng, unless teams can learn the organization cannot learn. In education discussions today, a learning culture within the school is a common topic of concern. The matter of contemporary importance is vested in the question, "To what extent are Seng's contentions in place in our discussions of a learning culture in schools?"

GARETH MORGAN AND SINGLE- AND DOUBLE-LOOP LEARNING

The foregoing question relative to Seng's fifth dimension concepts might well be promoted by the implementation of Gareth Morgan's concepts of double-loop learning. Single-loop learning, in brief, begins with scanning the environment and sensing its present operating norms and status. Step 2 includes the comparison of information in step 1 against operating norms that need correction. The process of initiating appropriate action is completed in step 3. However, the question as to whether or not the operating norms are appropriate has not been addressed.

Double-loop learning, according to Morgan, includes the process of questioning whether or not operating norms are appropriate for the situation being addressed. Double-loop learning strategies support the self-adjustment of practices by determining the "best" or appropriate norms for the present situation. Such a concept holds important implications for system design and the leadership roles that must be in place within the system.

In one of our limited and somewhat unscientific visits with practicing school administrators, consideration of such strategies as double-loop learning were never mentioned by them in their practices. Primary consideration was given to the matter of the school's vision and, in some cases, how that vision might best be implemented in the school program. It is noted that, at the time of such principal visitations, the topic of local control and federal curricular mandates, such as the Cardinal Principles, were in force in many school districts nationally and controls as to the matters of what is to be taught and how it should be taught were directing K–12 program practices.

ORGANIZATIONAL SUCCESS WITH FIVE CENTRAL CHARACTERISTICS: CRITICAL THINKING OF MICHAEL FULLAN

Space does not permit us, specifically, to set forth the many thoughts of Michael Fullan on education generally and on organizational success. Fullan is a Canadian and educational thinker/researcher who has shared his expertise with a wide variety of groups and organizations. He is widely recognized as an authority on educational reform and his research on what it takes for organizations to reach its efforts toward success.

In 2001, Fullan examined a number of successful cases in business and education in order to learn if these two entities had any common characteristics when it came to successful attainment of the organizations goals and objectives. He answered the question with a "strong yes" and set forth five central characteristics that underscored a successful result.

The five central characteristics of success were identified as follows: (1) a strong sense of moral purpose (make special note of the words moral and purpose); (2) an understanding of the change process (yes, but what understandings are of paramount importance? We discuss this need in the following section of the chapter); (3) well-developed relationship skills (but isn't this contention easier said than done?); (4) a capacity to facilitate knowledge sharing (once again, collaboration, cooperation, and communication come to the top); and (5) the ability to help the working group achieve coherence and connectedness (let's not forget the contributions of Mary Parker Follett and others in the development of the knowledge and skills needed to accomplish this end.).

NEW DAYS AND NEW WAYS TOWARD ORGANIZATIONAL EFFECTIVENESS

Constituent needs, new ways, problem-solving strategies, employee empowerment plus Theory Z, and pleasing the constituencies served as the primary motivation for the development of Deming's TQM concepts (1982) and Ouchi's Theory Z (1981) during this era of theoretical contentions. Total Quality Management was designed to serve businesses with emphasis given to "pleasing" the constituents whom the business was attempting to serve. This customer-focused strategy called for focusing on and meeting the specific needs of an organization. Secondly, special attention is to be given to resolve the dissatisfaction that has developed within the organization. That is, give full attention to the removing of worker dissatisfaction that has been caused by the status quo that been in place. New ways to do this and new ways to perform that and new ways to meet new goals are searched for and implemented within the organization.

In turn, new ways of assessing and evaluating present problem-solving strategies are developed and implemented. Organizational goals are viewed as continuously expanding rather than being ends in themselves. Worker empowerment is a fourth strategy that accompanies the TQM concept. Workers are directly involved in helping to establish the work to be accomplished but also are responsible for establishing the best methods and resources needed to complete the work successfully. That is, top-down control of worker activities is set aside for fostering worker initiative and responsibility for the work to be done.

William Ouchi (1981) and his Theory Z concepts contributed a great deal to the reconstructionist movement by placing emphasis on participative management, consensus decision-making, and reduced bureaucracy within the organization. We note that the previous discussion of McGregor's Theory Y and Likert's Type 4-T organizational model, to be discussed next in chapter 4, underscores the importance of a positive organizational climate similar to that of Ouchi's Theory Z. Theory Z places an emphasis on *subtlety* by studying the matter at hand and basing decisions on these findings as opposed to using the inflexible rules that do not give room for positive personal judgments and innovative ideas.

In addition, *intimacy* that is exemplified by the interpersonal relationships practices within an organization serves to foster a positive social community that centers on the problems and needs of others. The practice of viewing a situation from the perspective of the other persons accompanies intimacy in building the essential characteristic of *trust* in the organization. Without trust, communication, collaboration, and communication cannot be effectively developed within the organization.

LIKERT'S SYSTEM 4-T ORGANIZATION—A STEP HIGHER THAN SYSTEM 4

Likert's System 4-T system of organization was discussed briefly earlier in the chapter. System 4-T included certain positive characteristics that when beyond those of System 4. In system 4-T, a higher level of technical knowledge and skill is required along with a higher level of cooperative activity and interunit membership is planned for the improvement of working relationships. Intergroup membership is exemplified when on a member of one school committee/group also sits with a different school committee/group for purposes of communication and collaboration. Reportedly, the results of increased productivity and organizational benefits, fewer troublesome problems, and higher levels of worker cooperation are witnessed in the 4-T system.

Give a moment's thought to the characteristics of system 4-T. How many of the foregoing characteristics of system 4-T might you be able to identify that are in place in your school or one in which you are most familiar? For example, is the concept of interunit membership practiced in the program activities in the school system that you know about? If so, just how is this strategy being implemented in the school program that you might be considering? Is a high level of worker cooperation being practiced? Are there on a few troublesome problems having to be faced within the school and/or school system?

THEORIES AND CONCEPTS RELATED TO STUDENT LEARNING STYLES

Most commonly, theories/concepts about student learning styles have focused on four different ways that students learn best. The basic idea is that the teacher should assess the best of these four learning styles and use those methods to gain the best learning outcomes for the individual student. Visual or spatial learners are ones that prefer pictures, images, and other spatial resources to facilitate learning. Aural learners achieve best when auditory methods are utilized. Listening and using musical sound serve some students best. Verbal or linguistic learners prefer the spoken word and writing. Thus, lectures, discussions, and other forms of verbal teaching serve the verbal learner best. The kinesthetic or physical learner learns best by using the body, hands-on involvement, and related physical connections with the lesson at hand.

Learning theory does have its acceptance by various authorities and there are other theoretical models that focus on how the human mind works.

Anthony Gregorc (1984) set forth his model of learning styles that presents concepts termed *perceptual quality* and *ordering ability.* His interesting model provides an organized way for considering how the human mind actually works. He notes that mind styles are classified under the perceptual quality as being concrete or abstract.

Concrete quality registers information through one's senses of sight, smell, touch, taste, and hearing. Gregorc contends that this quality one is dealing with the "here and now" or the making of relationships between ideas or concepts. On the other hand, abstract quality enables one to visualize and understand what is not actually experienced or seen. Such factors as imagination and intuition come into play. Gregorc states that is common for an individual to have both of these qualities to some extent, but a person tends to use one of them more frequently than another.

Ordering ability has two dimensions, sequential and random. Sequential ability allows the individual to organize information logically. It is viewed as being linear in that it allows one to organize information by using a logical train of thought. Setting forth a plan is preferred to moving ahead on a matter without much thought. *Random* ability allows the individual to organize information in different ways or being more anxious to move ahead rather than taking time to plan.

Thus, the four ordering abilities are present in each person but Gregorc contends that the individual commonly uses one ability more than another. Each person has a unique combination of natural strengths and abilities. As stated by Gregorc (1969, 1984). "No one is a 'pure' style." Each of us has a unique combination of natural strengths and abilities. Four combinations of the strongest perceptual and ordering ability in each individual are viewed under the titles of: (1) Concrete Sequential (CS); (2) Abstract Random (AR); (3) Abstract Sequential (AS); and (4) Concrete Random (CR).

The following section sets forth the behavioral/learning characteristics of one of the four styles, the Abstract Random style:

The Abstract Random Style
The learner likes
- to listen to others,
- bringing harmony to group situations,
- establishing healthy relationships with others,
- focusing on the issues at hand.

They learn best when
- in a personalized environment,
- given broad or general guidelines,
- able to maintain friendly relationships,
- able to participate in group activities.

What's hard for them?
- having to explain or justify feelings,
- competition,
- working with dictatorial/authoritarian personalities,
- working in a restrictive environment,
- work with people who don't seem friendly,
- concentrating on one thing at a time,
- giving exact details,
- accepting even positive criticism.

(Anthony Gregorc, 1969, 1984, *Mind Styles—Anthony Gregorc*)

Give consideration to how the foregoing knowledge would be of benefit to the teacher in grades K–12. We contend that such knowledge would serve the learning culture of the school in many ways. Just how well known it is and whether or not it is being implemented in K–12 schools nationally are not known. The work of Gregorc was not known by any of the school personnel in one of our elementary school visitations nor was it included in the preparation programs for teachers or administrators in one major university in the southwest. We must make note of the fact that no major survey was completed to "investigate" this matter.

As is the case with so many of the theories and concepts set forth historically, the theory by name might not be programmed in school settings but certain concepts of the theory might be in place in many classroom instructional strategies.

COMPETENCY-BASED PROGRAMMING: LEARNING NOT TIME IS THE BASIC FEATURE

As early as the 1960s, innovative teacher and administrator educational programs were introduced in U.S. higher education. Since that time, competency-based concepts have been implemented in degree programs, training programs, development programs, evaluation and assessment strategies, staffing decisions, performance management, compensation practices and other programs and activities in business, industry, and educational programs. As reported by the American Compensation Association of Scottsdale, Arizona in 1996, competencies are increasingly what make the world go around.

Contemporary applications of competency-based concepts are being practices to guide personnel decisions, implement employee development programs, assess worker performance, and implement organizational compensation practices. Specifically, one primary application of competency-based programming centers on hiring decisions. In addition, pay for performance plans have been put into practice by a growing number of business corporations.

Nearly two decades ago, Norton (2002) published a competency-based performance program that set forth the specific competencies and their related indicators for K–12 school principals, human resources directors, instructional leaders, and other administrative personnel. He defined the term *competency* as having the knowledge and skill to accomplish a specific task as a desired level of success. An *indicator of competency* was viewed as a behavior that actually demonstrates the ability to perform a task at the desired level. Indicators of competency commonly are viewed as being measurable in terms of quality and purpose.

Laskaris (no date, four years ago) suggested four basic rules to follow in setting up and implementing a competency-based training program for adults: Rule 1; Measure employee learning rather than time; Rule 2; Harness the power of technology for teaching and learning; Rule 3; Shift the focus from the trainer to the trainee; and Rule 4; Align competencies with assessments. This example represents just one of the contemporary applications of competency-based programming that came into play nearly six decades ago.

Table 4.2 sets forth an example of one selected administrative task for a K–12 school leader. The task is specified along with several examples of behaviors that indicate competency for the administrator in practice.

Table 4.2 Task and Related Competencies for a School Leader

Task	Competencies
Task 1.0 To take the leadership role for the development of an effective curricular program and instruction-al procedures that meet the needs and interests of all students.	1.1 Ability to establish priorities in conjunction with student needs, district requirements, and state regulations. 1.2 Ability to involve students, teachers, and parents in establishing and maintaining curricular goals and objectives. 1.3 Ability to organize, supervise, and evaluate programs in relation to stated purposes. 1.4 Ability to assess teacher talent and utilize it in leadership and followership situations to meet stated objectives. 1.5 Ability to assess student needs and interests in relation to program design and instructional methods determined by staff per-personnel, parents, and students.

WHATEVER HAPPENED TO THE ISLLC STANDARDS FOR SCHOOL LEADERS?

More than two decades ago, The National Council for Teacher Education (NCATE) and the Inter-State School Leaders Licensure Consortium (ISLLC) set forth six standards for school leaders that "swept" the country for several years. By the year 2004, some forty states had adopted the standards for improving the preparation programs for the licensing of school leaders. Local school administrators soon caught on to the related themes of these standards; all children can learn, no child should be left behind and the promotion of developing a learning culture within each and every school.

These standards could be viewed as a paradigm or model for educational programs. For example, ISLLC standard number 1, as did all other standards, focused on knowledge: learning goals in a pluralistic society, developing a strategic plan, systems theory, information sources, effective communication, and effective consensus building and negotiation skills. ISLLC standard number 2 stresses the leader's responsibility for promoting the success of all students by advocating, nurturing, and sustaining a school culture and instructional program conducive to student learning and staff professional growth.

The standards were criticized by some authorities for their limitations relative to a comprehensive perspective of the work of school leaders, as previously noted, the standards received wide attention by school districts nationally for several years. Should the federal government or other agencies determine the educational standards for local school? The control of education by external agencies was strongly contended by local groups and individuals. ISLLC and such programs as common core came under high scrutiny by teacher and administrative groups across the nation.

Should all students be expected to perform at the same level? Isn't standard-based learning contrary to fairness and the fact that all students are different? Don't learning standards tend to erase the important characteristic of initiative and creative leadership in local school programs? Do not the local teachers and school administrators in the best position to determine the educational needs and interest of their students?

Although many of the concepts recommended by the ISLLC standards are included in the behaviors of contemporary school administrators, their specific identification is seldom recognized today. For example, aren't the standards of effective communication, student growth and development, the values of diversity and its meaning for educational programs, human resources administration, professional code of ethics and other such standards important considerations for educational programming nationally?

94   Chapter 4

MEASUREMENTS AND FORMULAS
FOR DETERMINING RESULTS

Education and educational administration have witnessed a wide variety of formulas for comparing or demonstrating the status or conditions of a variety of practices. These formulas might correctly be placed under the title of paradigms since they do represent models for demonstrating certain relationships and study results.

For example, Harl Douglass (1928) developed the first formula for determining the work load of a secondary school teacher. Later, in 1992, Norton and Bria developed a formula for measing the workload of an elementary school teacher. In 1962, Halpin and Croft set forth the Organizational Climate Description Questionnaire that has been used in numerous climate studies in schools across the nation. The contingency leadership octants set forth by Fiedler and Chemers (1974) might be viewed as a paradigm or model as well.

Although the workload of teachers is a common topic in discussions of educational problems and conditions, with the exception of Douglass' high school teacher load and Norton and Bria's elementary teacher load formulas, little or no attention has been given to the improvement of this matter. The Douglass load formula has revealed the fact that in many school settings at the secondary school level, teachers with the highest teacher load can be as much as three times that of other teachers with the lowest work load.

In addition, Norton (1959) found that the "best" teachers and teachers in their first year of teaching have been found to carry the heaviest teaching loads. The result is that the performance of the best teachers can be reduced to a level of actual mediocrity. Teacher turnover statistics reveal that, among the 20 percent of teachers that leave their school system after the first year of teaching, the majority are teachers with high potential.

WHAT CONSTITUTES TEACHER LOAD?

Class size is often equated with the term teacher load. In fact, class size is only one major factor that makes up the total load index of a teacher. Other load factors are the number of subject matter preparations required, the length of the class periods, the nature of the subject being taught, the nature of the students being taught, and the extracurricular duty assignments performed. It is beyond the scope of chapter 4 to discuss the calculation of teacher load in-depth. However, the formula (model) for determining the load index of a secondary school teacher is shown as follows:

The Douglass Teacher Load Formula

$$TL = SGC [CP - DUP/10 + (NP - 25 \, CP/100)]$$

$$[(PL + 50/100) + 0.6PC (PL = 50/100)]$$

SCG is the given subject grade coefficient,
CP is the number of class periods of the teacher per week,
DUP is the number of duplicate classes per day for the teacher,
NP is the number of students instructed by the teacher each day five days a week,
PL is the length of the class periods,
PC is the calculation of the teacher's cooperative duties.
(Note: For further explanation of the Douglass formula and the calculation of load see: (Human Resources Administration for Educational Leaders, Norton, 2008, Sage Publications)).

Unfortunately, the use of the Douglass load formula or the Norton/Bria elementary teacher load formula is seldom put into practice in contemporary schools. Commonly, load is determined primarily by class size and the number of classes taught each day. If school has six class periods daily, it is most common that a teacher will teach five classes daily with one preparation period daily. Some attention is given to class size, but this one load factor depends on the school board policy that generally specifies the maximum class size for most academic subjects. Why do so many professionals leave teaching so early in their educational career? Salary? Mandates? Peer relationships? Student relationships? District policy and administration? Technical supervision? Other personal reasons? We add Teacher Work Load!

CONCLUDING COMMENTS

The primary purpose of chapter 4, as stated at the outset of the chapter, was to present selected theories/concepts that followed the human relations era with emphasis on the practice of administrative leadership and organizational practices. We believe that the content in chapter 4 meets the purpose relative to selected theories/concepts that were set forth during the postmodern era. In fact, the number and variety of theories proved to be what could rightly be termed "overwhelming." It is realized that many important theories that have implications for educational practice were not included in the book. Numbers simply were beyond the scope of the book.

Meeting the second intended purpose of the chapter, that of determining the extent of a theory's implementation in educational practice, was not so easy to address. We have learned that many theories have found their way into education and benefited educational practices as a result. In most cases, however, theories have tended to make their mark on education in some way. The most beneficial ideas been absorbed into practice, but other ideas have tended to fall through the cracks of ever-changing time. In some cases, an early developed theory served as the basis for extending a new concept. Many innovative ideas such as Gantt's early chart models have been extended in some fashion into most every operating organization in operation today.

By over stretching the implementation rationale, it seems logical to suggest that each one of the many leadership theories is being practiced by some K–12 school leader in some school in America. Most likely, the leader doing so would not be able to name the "theory" that he or she is implementing, but the concepts are most beneficial. We submit that few of our many effective school leaders would be able to cite the "given name" of the leadership type that they think they are employing. It isn't that these leaders do not know the general differences between democratic or autocratic leadership or perhaps the differences between the characteristics of a nomothetic leader or an idiographic leader, but perhaps are leading by actually implementing the characteristics of these leadership styles.

Theories that focus on human motivation, student learning, job satisfaction, organizational development, human resources administration, and other educational fields of practice, in some way and some form are using concepts that they have learned in preparation programs, observation, and personal experience to be effective for them in their professional roles. We submit that, if the leadership or teaching principles were assessed and evaluated for any practicing education professional, that one could relate these characteristics to one or more theories that have been set forth by some "authority" sometime in history. Does theory influence contemporary practices in teaching and admiration. We are confident that the answer is "definitely yes."

KEY CHAPTER IDEAS AND RECOMMENDATIONS

- New concepts relating to organizational management and organizational development ranged widely during the postmodern era. The topic of organizations, including schools, as being social systems dominated the thinking in a variety of ways. The concept that all organizations consist of two primary dimensions, the structural and the human, dominated much of the theoretical

work of authorities during this time period. Even in this case, however, the concept of schools as social systems came under certain scrutiny during this era. Such criticism focused mainly on the concept of social systems due to its apparent oversight of external influences on educational purposes and programs.
- The topic of leadership continued its presence in theory development during this era. Contingency leadership, transformational leadership, aesthetic leadership, heterarchical leadership, contingency leadership, and others were among the leading theories set forth for implementation in K–12 administrative programs.
- Leadership behavior turned its attention to the school and its learning culture. Heterarchical leadership underscored the characteristics of initiative, self-organization, flexibility, and self-learning. These and other creative concepts are being witnesses in the reframing of educational programming in many school districts in America today.
- Decision-making continued to be a topic of concern during this era. Double-loop learning, for example, as proposed by Morgsan, recommended that more attention be given to assessing whether or not operational norms, presently in place, were appropriate for the situation being addressed.
- Morality came into the picture making a case for success in organizational operations. Ethics, trust, honesty, and positive relationships were viewed as being of paramount importance in determining an organization's effectiveness and success.
- Although somewhat debated, student learning styles were conceptualized as being evident and important for K–12 teachers to know and practice. The principle of "knowing your students" meant far more than just knowing their names and family relations. How each student learns best was presented as an important responsibility of teacher personnel.
- Competency-based concepts became highly visible once again during this era. Competency-based education, competency-based instruction, competency-based performance, competency-based compensation, and mostly everything else tended to focus on knowledge/skill, implementation, and practice as the road to success. Similar to the term efficiency during the scientific management era, competency-based education came to be viewed as the sin qua non of successful performance.
- Matters, such as teacher workload, historically been a topic of concern in educational improvement conversations. Teacher burnout, retention, job satisfaction, and teaching performance have been discussed at length over the years. Teacher workload has commonly been stated as the reason for various negative results. Although there have been strategies available to school leaders for many years to deal with the negative outcomes of load inequities, no serious attention has been directed to their implementation.

We view this oversight as a primary failure of professional personnel leading our schools.

DISCUSSION QUESTIONS: SELF-ASSESSMENTS

1. Re-read the "concluding comments" set forth in chapter 4. What are your thoughts regarding the impact of theory on educational practices?
2. Assume that you are participating in a session with teachers and administrators on the topic of professional preparation for positions in education. One participant states, "My higher education classes were too theoretical to be of much value. More experience on the job is what is needed for potential teachers and administrators." How might you respond to this contention?
3. Give thought to an administrator that you have known and considered as being one of the best leaders that you have experienced. Give several reasons why you reached that point of view. That is, what specific leadership characteristics did that leader demonstrate? In turn, what leadership style set forth in chapter 4 best reflects the leadership characteristics set forth in chapter 4? Are the characteristics that you identified mostly affective (kindness, fairness, supportive, etc.) or mostly cognitive (knowledgeable, skilled, intelligent, etc.)?
4. The topic of aesthetic leadership sets forth "new thinking" about the nature of leadership and why its characteristics loom important in educational practice. Review the information in chapter 4 regarding aesthetic leadership and then explain its significance to a group of aspiring educational administrators in a higher education preparation program.
5. Give thought to your personal life experiences as a "leader" in a club, committee, organization, or other school community activity. Looking back on these experiences, how successful was your leadership in achieving the stated goals and objectives of the group?

How might you have improved your leadership performance? What primary theories/concepts would characterize your leadership style at the time? What information set forth in chapter 4 would have been most helpful to you for improving your leadership style?

REFERENCES

Bogue, G. (1985). *The Enemies of Leadership: Lessons for Leaders in Education*. Bloomington, IN: Phi Delta Kappa Education Foundation.

Burns, J. M. (1971). *Leadership.* New York: Harper & Row.

Deming, W. E. (1982). *Out of the Crisis.* Cambridge, MA: The MIT Press, Massachusetts Institute of Technology.

Douglass, H. R. (1928). "Measuring Teacher Load in the High School." *The Nation's Schools* 2, no. 4: 22–24.

Duke, D. L. (1986). "The Aesthetics of Leadership." *Education Administration Quarterly* 22, no. 1: 7–27. Thousand Oaks, CA: Sage Journal.

Etzioni, H. (1975, 1997). *A Comprehensive Analysis of Complex Organizations.* Rev. ed. New York, NY: Free Press.

Fiedler, F. E., and Chemers, M. M. (1974). *Leadership and Effective Management.* Glenview, I. L.: Scott, Foresman.

Fullan, M. (2001). *The Meaning of Educational Change.* London: Routledge.

Getzels, J. W., and Guba, E. G. (1957). "Social Behavior and the Administration Process." *School Review* 65: 423–441.

Greenfield, T. B. (1974, July). *Theory in the Study of Organizations and Administrative Structures: A New Perspective.* A paper presented at the Annual Meeting of the International Intervisitation Programme on Educational Intervisitation (3rd), Bristol, England.

Gregorc, A. F. (1969, 1984). *Energetic Models of Styles.* From the web: https://web. cortland. ed/andearsmd/learning/Gregorc.htm.

Likert, R. (1979). "From Production and Employee Centeredness to System T-4." *Journal of Management* 5: 147–157.

Lunenburg, F. C. (2012). *Power and Leadership: An Influence Process, vol. 15, no. 1.* Houston,TX: Sam Houston State University.

McGregor, D. (1960). *The Human Side of Enterprise.* New York: McGraw-Hill.

Morgan, G. (1987). *Images of Organization.* Newbury Park, CA: Sage.

Norton, M. S. (1959). *Teacher Load in Nebraska High Schools in Cities from 5,000 to 25,000 Populations.* An unpublished doctoral dissertation, University of Nebraska at Lincoln, Nebraska. Department of Educational Administration and Supervision. Lincoln, NE.

Norton, M. S. (1992). "Toward an Equitable Measure of Elementary School Teacher Load." *Record in Educational Administration and Supervision* 13, no. 1: 62–66.

Norton, M. S. (2008). *Human Resources Administration for Educational Leaders.* Lanham, MD: Rowman & Littlefield.

Ouchi, W. (1981). *Theory Z: How Ameriacan Business can meet the Japanese Challenge.* Reading, MA: Addison-Wesley.

Seng, P. (1990). *The Fifth Dimension: The Art and Practice of the Learning Organization, vol. 30, no. 5,* p. 37. New York: Doubleday.

Stodgill, R. M. (1974). *Handbook of Leadership: A Survey of Leadership Theory and Research.* New York: Free Press.

About the Author

Dr. **M. Scott Norton** has served as a secondary school teacher of mathematics, coordinator of curriculum for the Lincoln, Nebraska School District; assistant superintendent for instruction; and superintendent of schools in Salina, Kansas, before joining the University of Nebraska as professor and vice chair of the Department of Educational Administration and Supervision. Later he served as a professor and chair of the Department of Educational Administration and Policy Studies at Arizona State University, where he is currently professor emeritus.

His primary research and instruction areas include educational leadership, human resources administration, teaching methods, governance policy, the assistant school principalship, competency-based administration, the school principalship, research methods, organizational development, organizational change, organizational development, organizational climate, and educational program improvement. He has published widely in national journals in the areas of teaching/instructional methods, organizational climate, gifted student programs, great teachers, student retention, organizational change, and others. He has published widely on a variety of educational topics for Rowman and Littlefield Publishers.

Dr. Norton has received several state and national awards honoring his services and contributions to the field of education and educational administration including awards from the American Association of School Administrators, the University Council for Educational Administration, the Arizona School Administrators Association, the Nebraska School Administrators Association, the Arizona Educational Research Association, Arizona State College of Education Dean's Award for Distinguished Service to the Field, and the Arizona Information Service, and the award for service as the president of the College of Education Faculty Association. He presently is serving as a member of the Arizona State University Emeritus College.

Dr. Norton's state and national leadership positions have included service as executive director of the Nebraska Association of School Administrators, member of the board of directors for the Nebraska Congress of Parents and Teachers, president of the Nebraska Council of Teachers of Mathematics, president of the Arizona School Administrators Higher Education Division, and member of the Arizona School Administrators Board of Directors, staff associate for the University Council for Educational Administration, treasurer of the University Council for School Administration, state representative for the Nebraska Association of Secondary School Principals, member of the Board of Editors for the American Association of School Public Relations, and council member for the Arizona State University Emeritus Council.

www.ingramcontent.com/pod-product-compliance
Lightning Source LLC
Chambersburg PA
CBHW030146240426
43672CB00005B/297